Respect

Citizenship through RE & PSE

Ina Taylor

Published in 2003 by:
Nelson Thornes Ltd
Delta Place
27 Bath Road
CHELTENHAM
GL53 7TH
United Kingdom

03 04 05 06 07 / 10 9 8 7 6 5 4 3 2 1

A catalogue record for this book is available from the British Library

ISBN 0 7487 6829 7

Edited by Katherine James

Picture research by Sue Sharp

Illustrations by Lisa Berkshire, John Harman and Peters & Zabransky

Page make-up by Vicky McFarlane Design

Printed and bound in China by Midas Printing International Ltd

Acknowledgements
With thanks to the following for permission to reproduce photographs and other copyright material in this book:

Amnesty International, p 87; Andes Press Agency/Carlos Reyes-Manzo, pp 18, 49, 65, 67, 88 (bottom), 89, 90; Barnado's, p 19; Benetton UK Ltd, p 76; Anthony Blake Photo library/Sue Darlow, p 28; Art Directors and Trip, pp 38, 39, 45; Associated Press, pp 46, 73; CAFOD, p 37; CAFOD/Duncan Green, p 36; Centre for Alternative Technology, p 57; ChildLine, pp 18, 23; Children's Society, p 47; Football Unites, Racism Divides, p 74; Mike Gunnill, p 82; Iwan Jones, p 13 (top); Impact Photos/Lionel Derimais, p 43; John Birdsall Photography, pp 17 (inset), 25, 35 (inset), 48, 68, 77, 87 (right), 88 (top); Oxfam, p 13 (bottom); Press Association, p 63; Professional Footballers Association, p 75; Rex Features Limited, p 80 (top); Rex Features Limited/Peter Hosking, p 87 (left); Rex Features Limited/PNS, p 69; Rex Features Limited/Simon Ryder, p 72; Rex Features Limited/Sipa, p 61; Rex Features Limited/Today, p 21; Rex Features Limited/Tony Kyriakou, p 59; Martin Sookias, pp 5 (top), 7 (top), 41, 71; Still Pictures/David Drain, p 9; Still Pictures/UNEP, cover; Ina Taylor, pp 26, 29, 31, 32, 34, 56; Trade Justice Movement, pp 91, 92

Every effort has been made to contact copyright holders. The publishers apologise to anyone whose rights have been inadvertently overlooked, and will be happy to rectify any errors or omissions.

Contents

Introduction – that's life!

Lots of the things you study in RE are connected with people – what they do and why they do it. It can be very hard to separate subjects into different drawers and make them stay there. Like life, everything is interconnected. RE can't be filed comfortably in one drawer, either. When you are discussing the creation theories of various religions, in no time you are into the Big Bang theory and evolution. Suddenly it sounds like a science lesson and you need to check facts with that department. Work on the environment rapidly moves into Geography and possibly Science again. It is not surprising to find that Citizenship, which concerns itself with who we are and how we respect one another and our environment, should turn up in RE, but also puts in an appearance in Geography, Maths, English, PSE – indeed every subject on the curriculum. This is because Citizenship is concerned with life on a personal, local, national, international and even global level.

You may begin working on a topic in RE, but don't be afraid to let it wander across into another subject if necessary. Ask other departments in school for assistance and look for information and help wherever necessary.

In this book we are going to look at the topics in the Citizenship course using the skills developed in RE to understand what is going on and what, if anything, all this means for us as citizens of the 21st century. As well as getting a great deal of fun out of your involvement in issues, you will also develop new skills that will boost your confidence and will be of help to you in the future.

This is *active* Citizenship, so it is going to mean more than just reading this textbook. Most of the situations mentioned in the book are real and going on in the world at the moment. You need to understand why these things are happening, whether they will have any impact on you and what, if anything, you want to do about it. You don't have to sit here and just take it! As a citizen of this planet you have the right to be heard and to have your opinion considered. That might seem highly unlikely when the world's population stands at 6.2 billion and rising, but Citizenship shows you how you can do it. Have your say and make a difference!

Along with the facts and information in this book, there are also lots of suggestions for projects you might like to get involved with. There isn't time to develop everything, and some will appeal to you more than others. The teacher's file that accompanies this book contains other suggestions and, as you work, you or members of the group may well come across totally new issues that you feel strongly about.

Great! Follow them up. Get informed, then get active! Decide what you want to do about the issue. Pages 93–94 give you Top 10 Tips for getting active.

Make full use of ICT. It is fast, easy and cheap. You can use the internet to research facts about most things. All through this book you will find weblinks to help you in your internet research. They are shown by this icon: .

When you go to the Respect web page (www.nelsonthornes.com/respect) you will find the links for each unit. You can also email groups and organisations requesting more information, or find out about getting involved in their activities. The library is another vital resource with books and newspapers to support your research.

Don't just rely on what it says in books and newspapers! Check it out yourself. Contact organisations or individuals. Arrange to go and visit them if they are close enough, or perhaps conduct an interview on the phone or by email. Your school and your teacher need to be kept fully informed of this. It is not just for your security but because all your work forms part of the Citizenship course – and they will need to keep track of it, too. More tips on conducting interviews appear on page 94.

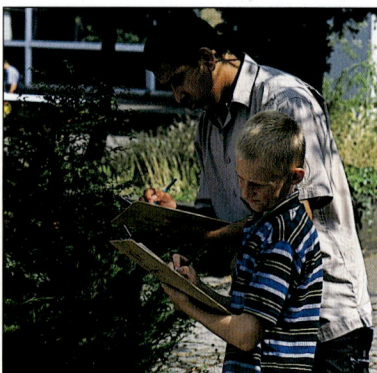

Active means just that. None of the units in this book can be fully explored by just reading them – you have to get out and do something. The student in this picture is completing a survey.

Don't forget to make full use of the media. The topics you are involved in are of interest to other people. Your local radio station may well be happy to feature your work or to invite you to talk about it. Don't be shy! Make contact with them, because you never know what doors may open for you as a result. If you are invited to do a spot, prepare for it carefully. Beforehand, write one sentence that sums up what you are interested in. Then, underneath, bullet-point the key parts of this. Nobody will mind if you take this with you on an A5-size card as a prompt.

Publicising your activities is another important part of Citizenship. You have a voice and a right to be heard. Not only can you talk about your ideas but you can put up displays that will reach a wider audience when you are busy somewhere else.

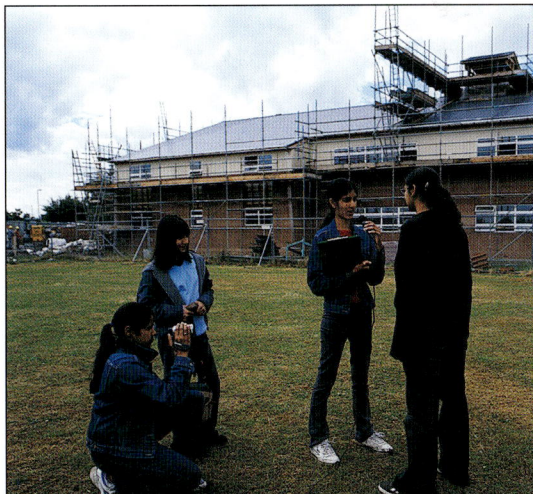

Keeping a record of your work is important. Don't limit yourself to paper. Photographs can make your work come alive, and a video presentation may be even better. If you are doing a presentation, try using prompt cards or an OHT to remind you what to say, rather than reading from a script. Make sure you introduce your topic so that your audience know what you are talking about, and summarise your points at the end. Don't forget to ask if anyone has any questions. You might even suggest to your friends beforehand some questions they could ask.

When you see this icon you know there are links to the web. Go to the 'Respect' webpage on **www.nelsonthornes.com/respect** which will link you to the best internet sites to help with your research.

It is important to be active! Check out material for yourself. Make up your own mind about the facts. That's what active citizenship is all about.

What a load of rubbish!

'God looked at everything he had made and he was very pleased.' (*Genesis 1:31*)

'For the sake of posterity, those countless generations of unborn children to come, let us save the Earth.' (*Guru Nanak*)

'Continue to contaminate your bed, and you will one night suffocate in your own waste.' (*Chief Seattle, a Native American, 1855*)

'God's creation is sacred. Humanity does not have the right to destroy what it cannot create.' (*Hindu statement on the environment*)

- Three of these four quotations represent three of the world's main religions. Which religions are represented by these quotations? What have Chief Seattle's words got to do with this picture? Could a rubbish dump harm anyone?

- Look at Friends of the Earth's website for details about landfill.

1.1 Stewardship

Christians, Muslims and Jews share the belief that humans were put on earth by God, who created everything. During the short time we live on the earth, we are free to use the earth's resources for our needs but when we die, we must hand the earth back in the same state we received it. The earth is not our property, we are just caretakers or guardians who look after the planet during our lifetime. The word 'stewardship' is used by these religions to mean this.

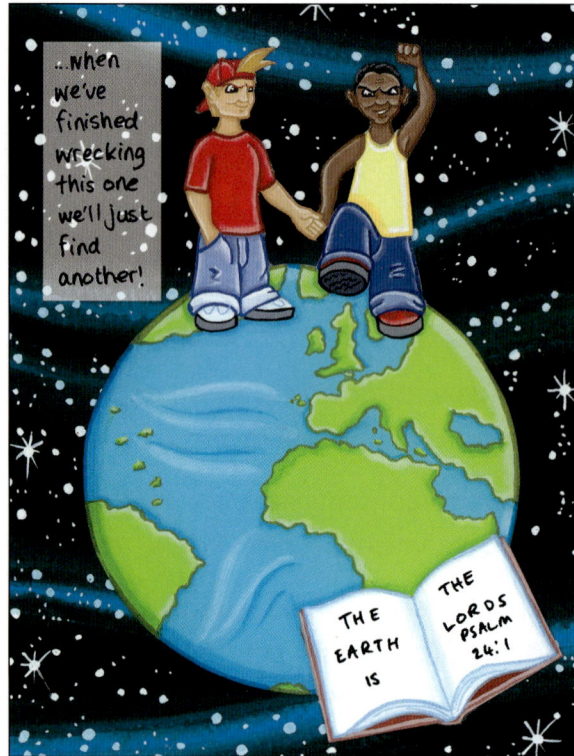

We are God's stewards and agents on earth. We are not masters of this earth; it does not belong to us to do what we wish. It belongs to God and He has entrusted us with its safekeeping. (*Muslim Declaration on Nature*)

I have a mental picture of people sharing a massive banquet completely oblivious to the fact that the roof is crumbling and will eventually come crashing down on their heads. There are other people standing at the exits warning the diners to leave, but they take no notice – the meal is too good. (*F M Khalid*)

With a partner

- Discuss with a partner what you think the connection is between this banquet and the rubbish tip on page 9.

- Use F M Khalid's idea of the banquet to plan a television advertisement for an environmental pressure group like Friends of the Earth. Include a storyboard.

An average dustbin contains 22.2 kg of rubbish per week.

Every year 2 million seabirds die from getting tangled in waste plastic, or eating it.

The UK recycles 11% of its rubbish; Switzerland recycles 50%.

Every person in the UK throws away four times their bodyweight in rubbish each year.

Burning rubbish creates toxic ash. In landfill sites this ash emits toxic gases.

Eight million disposable nappies are thrown away every day. These make up 4% of household waste.

Every 9 months the UK puts enough rubbish into landfill sites to fill Lake Windermere.

Landfill no longer means only burying rubbish underground. Today the word is used for waste mountains, too.

Every year we create 900,000 tonnes of electrical and electronic waste: 90% goes into landfill sites and it is responsible for 40% of the lead found in landfill sites. Lead is poisonous and gets into water supplies.

UK DUSTBIN

UK offices produce 15 million tonnes of waste a year. In the age of computers we actually now use more paper than ever – a third of a tonne per year for every person.

'Wheelie bins are wonderful, you can get so much in them.' As a result we now throw away far more than we ever did.

- Find out the policy of your local council on the disposal of household waste. Invite someone from the council to come and talk to the group about this issue. Be ready with questions about the collection, sorting and disposal of rubbish. Find out what percentage is being recycled. How do they plan to improve this?

- Research the use of incinerators for waste disposal. Use a spreadsheet to show the advantages and disadvantages of incineration over landfill. Friends of the Earth and Greenpeace have useful websites that you could consult for details. What else could be done with rubbish?

1.2 Resource or rubbish?

It is depressing to read about the problems created by rubbish. It is also tempting to believe we can't do anything about it – but that would be wrong. Environmental changes have come about in the past as a result of a few people taking a stand and encouraging others to follow. Lead was taken out of petrol and CFCs removed from aerosol cans as a result of public pressure.

Maybe we are looking at things in the wrong way.

Greenpeace says:

> Instead of accepting what our waste is and looking for ways to get rid of it, we should be asking why waste is produced and what it could become. As a source of pollution, rubbish needs to be controlled and hidden away. But treated as a resource it becomes a valuable material.

- What is the difference between treating waste as rubbish and treating it as a resource?

- Find out what 'green diesel' has got to do with this.

- List three reasons why a Christian might choose to use this container.

- Find out what sort of work the Salvation Army does – you could use their website. Could clothes have any part in that work?

- Find out what Oxfam does with the clothes that don't sell in their shops.

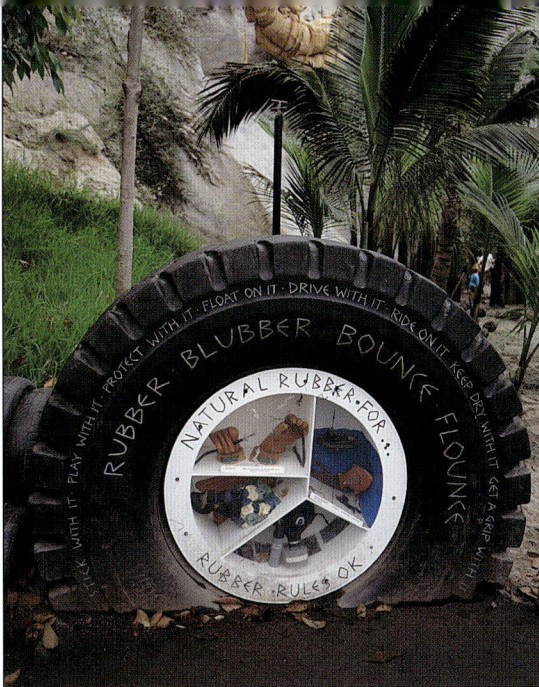

We throw away 100,000 tyres every day and it is thought that 200 million tyres litter our countryside. Yet rubber is a natural, useful resource. At the Eden Project in Cornwall, tyres have been cut in half to form comfortable benches – half makes the seat and half the back-rest. Tyres can also be made into crumb rubber to create springy surfacing for running tracks and children's playgrounds, and used for carpet underlay, too.

Did you know?

A dump of 10 million tyres in Knighton, Powys, caught fire in 1989 and has been smouldering ever since. It is now in the record books as the longest-ever burning tyre fire because it is still too hot for firefighters to tackle.

Oxfam has a campaign called 'bRing bRing' which recycles unwanted mobile phones.

In this country each individual ditches one mobile every 8 months. They contain hazardous chemicals which leak into the soil and watercourses around landfill sites.

Each old mobile is worth at least £5 to Oxfam who can use that money to support people all over the world. They say one old mobile enables Oxfam to provide a mosquito net to protect a child from malaria.

1.3 They've got it all wrapped up

We all love packaging. 'Don't judge a book by its cover,' they say, but we do. The advertisers know it, so a lot of time and money goes into the appearance of books and everything else we buy. Packaging is big business. In Britain it is worth £7.5 billion a year, and we seem quite happy to pay large amounts for something we will immediately throw away. Half the price of some foods goes in packaging. Make-up is even worse: a lipstick costs around £1 to manufacture but can sell for up to £10. To make people willing to pay that much, £2.50 is spent on advertising and £1.70 on packaging – the rest is profit!

- The UK uses 8 billion plastic bags a year.
- Most plastic bags are only used once.
- Most supermarket plastic bags last 10–20 years before they degrade.
- Most plastic bags end up in landfill sites.
- Ireland introduced a 9p tax on every new plastic bag. Pollution and waste in Ireland have dropped dramatically.
- 500 million plastic bottles are thrown away every year in the UK.
- 1.7 million tonnes of plastic are used every year to pack food and drinks.

- Looking at goods in a supermarket and amongst goods you have at home, investigate the number of layers of packaging of individual items. Some of the worst offenders can be prepacked fruit and vegetables, toiletries, cakes, sweets, meat and snacks. Don't forget that the person on the checkout may automatically bag some items as they scan them before the customer puts them into a plastic carrier.

- What were your three worst examples? Compare your list with those of others in the class. How essential was that packaging for food safety and hygiene?

The other side of the case

The British Plastic Federation says:

Plastics are amongst the most environmentally suitable materials for use in many packaging applications. Plastics are efficient because they are recyclable, they have low energy requirements in their manufacture and distribution and they do not pose pollution problems when incinerated.

Packaging without plastics would result in increases of 300% by weight, 150% by volume and 100% in energy consumption. By using plastic, up to 40% on food distribution fuel costs are saved, which in return reduces environmental pollution.

Is there an alternative?

Some supermarkets are already using biodegradable packaging. Instead of plastic, bags are made from potato starch or wheat starch. Check the policy of some leading supermarkets on this issue.

In Asia, rice husks, which don't burn, have begun to be used as a replacement for polystyrene packaging around electrical goods. The new packaging can be recycled again to use as a fireproof building material.

- Having read the various arguments on this page, what do you think should be done to prevent scenes like the one on page 9?

- Should religious people take an active part in campaigns about waste disposal? Why?

Debate this motion:

The government should put a tax of 10 pence on every item of plastic packaging.

Those giving their side of the argument could include:

- the owner of a factory making plastic containers for fast food
- a supporter of Friends of the Earth
- the owner of a very profitable landfill site
- a religious leader with three young children.

Unit 1 *feedback*

1 Make a model with a label, or a three-dimensional poster, out of rubbish collected around the school. The poster urges people to recycle rather than to dump. You need a catchy slogan.

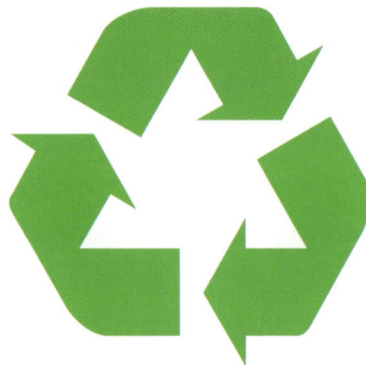

2 Write to your MP urging them to do more than talk about the UK's poor record on recycling, which at 11% is one of the worst in Europe. You would like to know what they are prepared to do about it that will result in action.

In groups

Choose a large supermarket and discover their policy on recycling and what they are doing to avoid excessive packaging. Go to their website for email contacts. Check your local branch of the store to see if there is evidence they are putting company policy into practice, particularly with their own-brand goods. Do you think the store is doing enough? What areas do you think could be improved?

As a class

Plan a thorough investigation into litter around the school. You need to find out the times when most litter is dropped, and the nature of the litter. Where are the products coming from? Who are the worst offenders? What is the school policy on litter? Is it working? What can be done to improve the situation? Record your investigations on a spreadsheet and present your recommendations in a report to the headteacher. The group Waste Watch has a useful website.

Who cares?

ChildLine believes that all children have the right to a safe childhood, free from abuse of any kind.

'We strive to offer comfort, advice and protection to any child or young person who seeks it from us, whatever their concern.

We also take what children tell us and relay it to the public and to decision-makers in order to improve children's lives.'

- List five sorts of problems you think ChildLine might deal with.

'A place in God's court can only be attained if we do service to others in this world.' (*Guru Granth Sahib*)

'The best house among the Muslims is the house in which an orphan is well treated and the worst house among the Muslims is the house is which an orphan is badly treated.' (*The Prophet Muhammad* ﷺ)

'And now I give you a new commandment: Love one another. As I have loved you, so you must love one another.' (*John 13:34*)

- Is there any reason why a religious believer might want to work for a charity like ChildLine?

Case studies

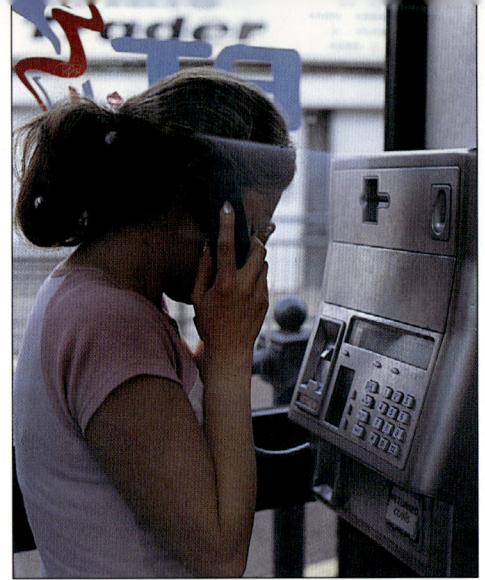

Jo first rang ChildLine when she was 14. She had been sexually abused by her grandfather from the age of 5 and she was desperate for it to stop but didn't know where to turn.

At first I couldn't talk about what was wrong. I gave the counsellor a rough idea, but it was impossible to tell her everything. The truth is that my grandpa was raping me — he had been for years, every time he came to baby-sit. And he had made me pregnant. I took an overdose but my parents found me. When I woke up in hospital, they wanted to know why but I couldn't tell them. I had a miscarriage because of the overdose.

My first call to ChildLine made me realise that there are people who care and want to make things better — and that I could do something to make it better too. I've been ringing regularly for the last four years and ChildLine has kept me going and really, really supported me. They never judged me about what went on.

1 Look at the table below. Find out how and when ChildLine started.

2 What action does ChildLine take when someone phones 0800 1111?

ChildLine
0800 1111

Problem area Age-group	Bullying	Abuse	Family relationships
Under 11	29%	23%	16%
12–15	15%	20%	16%
16–18	3%	16%	16%

3 Which problems seem to remain constant? Why do you think that is?

4 Which problems appear to get easier as people get older? Would you agree?

5 List four other problems you think callers of your age group might have been concerned about.

Barnardo's

GIVING CHILDREN BACK THEIR FUTURE

Ian was 16 when his father turned against him.

> He used to say I was stupid and useless; that I shouldn't be here. I tried to kill myself twice, but my dad said everything was my fault, even when he hit me.
>
> Ian left home but eight months later he lost his flat and job, had no contact with his parents and was addicted to drugs and alcohol. Police put him in touch with Barnardo's Bays project in Swansea, which found him temporary accommodation before helping him find and settle into his own flat. As well as providing practical help to homeless young people like Ian, the project helps them deal with other problems they may have as a result of their troubled past, such as addiction to drugs or alcohol. Ian, now 18, has his own flat, is starting a new job and has conquered his drug habit.
>
> 'I probably would have been dead by now if it wasn't for Barnardo's,' he says.

With a partner

1   It is estimated there are 33,000 homeless people aged 16–21 in Britain at the moment. Work out six reasons why that might happen to someone in your age group. Do you think this problem is worse than it was before? Why?

2   Look up Barnardo's website. What are their aims? Write a paragraph for a magazine about how the charity is helping black children who are excluded from school.

What are your rights?

In 1959 the United Nations set out the Declaration of the Rights of the Child. This stated that 'mankind owes the child the best it has to give'. Each child is entitled to:

✓ the right to an identity

✓ the right not to be discriminated against

✓ the right to equal treatment

✓ the right to family life

✓ the right to education

✓ the right not to be abused or exploited.

With a partner

1   Go through the points listed above and describe a situation where each of these is being violated. Arrange the list in order of importance. Why have you chosen that order?

2   Look back at Ian and Jo's cases on pages 18–19. Were their situations caused by any violations of their rights under the UN Declaration? If so, which?

3   Read the UN Declaration on the Rights of the Child in more detail on UNICEF's website. What right have you to an education? Why is that considered important?

4   What does 'the right to identity' mean? How has that clause recently affected the rights of people conceived as a result of artificial insemination by donor?

We care

- Like all religions, Islam takes the care of children very seriously. Find out what one Islamic charity – like Muslim Aid or the Red Crescent – does to help child victims of war. Then produce an A5 leaflet (double-sided) which gives a brief account of their work and accurate information about making a donation.

- Research the following charities to find out who founded them, when and why:

  > The Children's Society
  >
  > Barnardo's
  >
  > NSPCC

  Record your findings on a spreadsheet.

What similarities do you notice between the origins of these societies?

Why do you think they share similar beginnings?

What do you think are the advantages and disadvantages of a charity being connected to a specific religious group?

- There are many teachings in the Bible that Christians believe tell them to help people in need. Here are five such passages. Each member of your group should look up one or two of them. What do they say about helping people in need? Report back your findings to the group.

  - Luke 4:18–19
  - Romans 12:10–21
  - Matthew 18:5
  - Romans 13:9
  - Mark 10:13–16

Which of these passages do you think is likely to have the most influence on a Christian who is considering working for a children's charity? Why?

2.3 Number one stress

> **There is nowhere to get away from this torture.**

A teenager who was being bullied said:

> Some children are so traumatised that they have attempted suicide. There's evidence to suggest that half of all pupils may have been bullied at one time in their lives. (*Baroness Ashton*)

> Bullying was the biggest single problem that children rang us about last year – 22,372 children and young people rang ChildLine about this issue. (*Esther Rantzen, Chair of ChildLine*)

> One in every four teenagers has been a victim of bullying via a computer or mobile phone. (*Findings of a report by National Children's Home*)

> Bullying has been going on since people can remember. It's part of human nature. However, we shouldn't believe it is something we can't do anything about. (*Helen Cowie, Research Professor at Roehampton University of Surrey*)

> A quarter of young people said that bullying was the number one stress in their lives. (*Survey by the charity Young Voice*)

In groups of three or four

Discuss the following and make your recommendations.

1   What ideas can you come up with to protect pupils from bullying by anonymous text-messaging in school?

2   How much does a bully enjoy an audience? Is the bystander who does nothing as much to blame as the bully?

3   How do you stop people saying it's 'grassing someone up' if they report bullying?

4   Which of the facts in the speech bubbles above did you find the most surprising? Why?

CHIPS

Since 1998, ChildLine has been running a ground-breaking initiative with schools. CHIPS – ChildLine in Partnership with Schools – has brought ChildLine into direct contact with over a thousand UK secondary schools already, and more are becoming involved with ChildLine all the time.

CHIPS endorses the view that children and young people can play a part in making changes to improve their own lives, can help each other, and have a right to be listened to and respected.

How can CHIPS help?

CHIPS develops a working relationship with young people and their schools, providing a range of services that includes:

- information about issues that affect young people
- resources such as leaflets and factsheets
- direct work in schools by ChildLine staff, such as workshops on bullying or racism
- opportunities for pupils to visit ChildLine and learn about its work
- conferences, reports and published articles which are a forum for young people's voices to be heard and acted upon
- fund-raising opportunities and help with organising fund-raising activities.

Peer support

CHIPS encourages schools and young people's groups to help young people set up projects run by them to tackle the issues they face, by providing:

- support
- training
- information and resources.

- Could your group raise money to help the work of ChildLine? If you want some weird and wacky suggestions, look at ChildLine's website page 'A–Z fund-raising ideas'. Organise one event the whole school would enjoy and which the charity would benefit from. Make sure you publicise the work of CHIPS.

- If you do a fund-raising activity for a charity, mount a display. Use photographs, and write a report of the event stating the amount raised. Include any publicity material the charity sent to you, and a copy of the letter they wrote thanking the school for the donation.

Groupwork

1   Try to arrange for a permanent display-board in school that tells students where they can get help. ChildLine is only one of the charities that helps – include information about three more. There may be some with local links for your area. Make sure the display is clear, gives phone numbers about whom to contact, and is up-to-date and accurate. You need to arrange a rota of people to be responsible for maintaining the noticeboard. Could you arrange for a speaker from one of the charities to talk to year groups? Look again at the information given in this unit and on the websites to decide which particular topics would be most helpful to each year group.

2   Design a survey of the sort of things that worry students in your year. This will need to be anonymous and carefully planned to avoid upsetting anyone. Build in a question to see if gender (being male or female) plays any part in the types of problems. Analyse the results – a spreadsheet is one way but you may need to write a paragraph of conclusions. The results might influence the type of material that goes on your school display-board, and the charities posted there.

3   Find out about the work of Kidscape, which says it is 'the only children's charity that focuses upon preventative policies'. Use their website to find out how this policy works with bullying.

4   Exams cause a lot of stress. Look on ChildLine's website for their fact sheet called 'Exam stress and how to beat it'. Use it to create a poster with 'Five Top Tips' that could be displayed in classrooms.

5   Prepare a tape for local radio about how your school is tackling the issue of bullying.

6   What is the advantage of CHIPS organising a project that is run by young people?

Let's party!

Everyone enjoys a party, so plan to hold one in school. As a group you will be:

- researching which religious event to celebrate
- planning everything – venue, catering, guest list, etc.
- working out how to make it pay its way
- enjoying the party yourselves
- reviewing the success of the event at the end.

- 'For 7 days you must not eat any bread made with yeast … Celebrate this festival at the appointed time each year.'
- It is the day when new robes are presented to the monks.
- We took boxes of food to the old people.
- After evening prayers we raced outside and began lighting the lamps. Soon the whole street glittered.
- After a month of fasting the new moon is eagerly awaited.

Which religion does each of these relate to? What are they celebrating? How do they do it?

3.1 Getting started – the research

This Divali party was held in a classroom and the walls were decorated with stories connected with it.

As a class you have to pick the best religious festival for the school to celebrate, so you will need to do some research. You need six groups in the class, each group taking one of the main world religions.

A spreadsheet may well be the best way of recording this data. Each group needs to find out:

- The names of two major festivals
- When the festivals next occur
- How the festivals are celebrated in the home and in the community
- Symbols involved with the religion or festival that might be used on any publicity material
- Special foods associated with each festival

When your group has finished the research, decide which festival would be better for a school party, and why. Plan a 5-minute presentation, which one member of your group can give to the whole class. Tell everyone the advantages of choosing your festival, as well as any disadvantages there might be.

Choosing the right one

Listen to each group's presentation. Have a class discussion about which seems to be the most suitable.

Points to consider:

■ The **timing** of this event is important. You obviously need a festival that is coming up in the near future. Equally you have to have enough time to organise the catering, guest list, publicity, etc. Check the school diary, too. You do not want your party to clash with exams or some other school event that will draw attention away from your party.

■ Links with the **local community** are good for the success of this project. They could boost your numbers, raise your profile in the community and may bring in donations of food, help or money. That's worth considering!

■ Is there a **minority religious group** in your community who would welcome this sort of event to foster better community relations?

■ Would there be any major difficulties getting **display materials** and **foods** or **making contacts with members of that faith group**? You want to make a success of this project, so it is worth being realistic from the outset.

Decision time – which is it to be? As a whole group you need to vote on the best festival to celebrate.

3.2 Sharing out the jobs 1

There are six key areas that need tackling, so you need six groups. These could be the same groups that worked together on a world religion, or you might like to re-group according to people's personal interests and skills. In the end everyone is reliant on each other – so you must work well as a group and as a whole class.

A parent donated these Indian sweets to an Eid party. They were cut up to make them go further.

Group 1 Research and contacts

- Find out more about the religious origins of your festival. Is there a story connected with it? Use internet sites as well as books to help you.

- How could parts of this be shown on a display at the party?

- Check whether anyone in the school community – pupil, teacher, classroom assistant, kitchen staff, cleaner or governor – belongs to this faith community.

- Find out where the nearest faith community is based. Who is the person to contact there?

- Contact the food technology department in school and any other likely departments for assistance. Would they consider helping with the event as one of their class projects?

- When the planning has moved on sufficiently for arrangements to be fixed, write to your faith community contact. Tell them what your class is planning, ask if they would be prepared to help you or would like to be involved, and try to arrange for some of your group to visit them.

- When the guest list is agreed, write and send out invitations.

- Keep the other groups in the class regularly updated with your progress.

Group 2 Planning and logistics

- Find a suitable venue to hold the party. What numbers are permitted in that room? What are the health and safety implications? Do you need to do a risk assessment? What costs are involved? You will need to liaise with Group 4.

- When the venue is agreed, you need to plan how it can be used to its best advantage. Where will guests enter? Where will the food be served? Where will the drinks be served? Will guests stand or sit to eat? Which will be the exit? You must make sure that the fire exits are kept clear of furniture at all times. You need to prevent a log-jam in any one area and to plan for the safe, comfortable and free movement of people.

- Your group is responsible for setting out the room beforehand. Liaise with Group 5 to find out their requirements for serving food and drink. Do they need to be near a door to fetch extra supplies? What items of furniture – for example tables and chairs – do they require? Arrange to fetch, set up and return what is needed.

- Arrange for particular people to be responsible for setting out and clearing up the room.

- Where in the room will you place bins and bin-bags for rubbish? They need to be easily accessible, and regularly collected, removed and replaced. Who will be responsible for that?

These girls are at a Hannukah party. Pupils made and cooked latkes which were served with a salad garnish, doughnut, satsuma and a drink for £1.

Sharing out the jobs 2

Group 3 Publicity

- Decide on the best logo or symbol to use on all publicity connected with the party. You need to liaise with Group 1 to find out what you can use that will not cause religious offence, and the best shape to write on or around.

- Is there a name or slogan you want to use to give the party a special identity?

- You need to design and produce posters and tickets – to prevent them from being fraudulently photocopied, you could consider producing them on red paper.

- You need to write a press release for the school newsletter and the local newspaper. Is there a free newspaper to which you could send the press release? Make contact with the local radio to see if one of your group can do an interview. Would any of the journalists like to attend the party and report on it?

- Take photographs and a video of the groups in the planning stages as well as during the actual event.

- Organise the best places to display posters. Appoint various people to keep an eye on the posters and replace any that are torn or damaged, and to take down and collect publicity material after the event.

- Organise the sale of tickets beforehand. They need to be easily available to pupils, staff and anyone outside school who might like to come. The success of ticket sales will be a measure of how effective your publicity campaign has been.

The girls dressed especially for the school Eid party. Cut-outs of decorated hands were used on all publicity and as part of the room decoration.

Group 4 Costings and finance

- You have to make this event pay its way. That doesn't mean you should have to make a profit, but you shouldn't lose money. People want to enjoy the party and feel they have had good value for money. Most of your guests will be pupils and they may not have much money, so it might be a good idea to start out assuming that everyone who attends will pay £1. That way you can get plenty of people to come.

- Venue – you need to work closely with Group 2 and urge them to find somewhere large but free, like the school hall or a large classroom.

- When you know the number that this room can safely hold, plan the correct number of tickets to sell, e.g. 100. (Don't forget to count the people who are serving and working at the party; do workers have to pay?) Advise Group 3 of the ticket price.

- From Group 3 find out what they need to spend on publicity materials (investigate ways of reducing these costs by using friends, talking to the art department, etc.).

- From Group 5 find out what table coverings (paper?), disposable plates, cups and cutlery they will need. What about rolls of paper towels – and don't forget the black bin-bags. Can the school provide any of these things?

- When you have listed all these costs, deduct them from your potential ticket sales and then inform Group 5 how much they can spend on food and drink.

- Your group has to pull together the money side of the event. To keep costs down, involve as many friends, parents and other departments in the school as you can. Most of the ticket money will go on food and drink.

- Keep regular accounts of spending throughout. Prepare a final balance-sheet at the end of the project.

31

3.4   Sharing out the jobs 3

Group 5 Catering

- You are responsible for feeding everybody, and this is the part of the party that will be remembered most, so you must make a good job of it!

- Liaise with Group 1. What sort of food is traditional at this festival? Is there any food that members of this religion do not eat? Find out what contacts have been made with the faith community. Has anyone there offered to help with the catering? Where do members of the faith community usually buy their festival food? Have there been any offers of food for the party?

- Check with Groups 3 and 4 on the number of tickets to be sold and the amount of money you will have to spend.

- Has Group 1 made contact with the food technology department or the PTA? Can you use their kitchens, sinks or ovens?

- Check on the health and safety regulations concerning catering for this sort of event.

- Now for the hard bit! Plan a selection of food that is not expensive, is appropriate to the festival and can be served on one plate and eaten with fingers. Avoid messy things that need cutlery, like rice. You might get ideas from some of the pictures in this unit.

- What will the guests drink, that is not too expensive and is appropriate? How many drinks will you allow per person?

- How will you ensure that the food is served quickly? What will stop people coming back for more?

At this Eid party Amrine used a tube of henna to decorate pupils' hands with mendhi. It is inexpensive and was very popular. The henna is left on the hand as long as possible to stain the skin, then washed off (see page 25). A deep orangey-brown design remains.

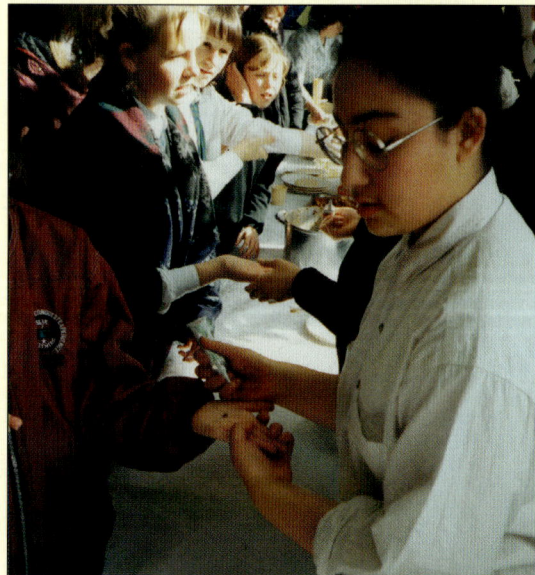

Group 6 Entertainment and decoration

- Check with Group 1 on the religious background to the festival. How can you interpret this on display-boards around the room? Does Group 1 have any contacts in the faith community who would loan posters or artefacts for display?

- What can you do to decorate the room (cheaply) in an appropriate manner for the religion, and to create an atmosphere of party celebration? Look at the picture on page 31.

- See if the art or geography departments will help. Does anyone else in the school have appropriate things like poetry, songs or videos?

- Is music, singing or dancing appropriate at this festival? If so, what can you arrange? Links with the faith community through Group 1 would be an advantage. Equally, working with the music or PE department might be helpful.

- Are there any other forms of entertainment or demonstrations that guests would enjoy? Are there any pupils in the school who could help with this? The picture opposite shows a pupil demonstrating mendhi, and there was no shortage of hands to work on.

Unit 3 *feedback*

It is worth looking back over the event and seeing what went really well, and looking at the things you would like to have done differently.

1   Arrange to stage a display of the party from the early planning to the end. Use photographs that were taken at each stage and add informative captions – or you could arrange a showing of the video that was made of the preparations and the event.

2   Write and thank everyone who played a part – especially people outside the immediate school community.

This Divali party was a great success. Everyone had a plate of food and a drink of lemonade for £1. A total of 150 tickets were sold, and there was even a small profit.

Groupwork

3   One representative from each of the six groups should give the class a brief report of the group's activities. What was the hardest part of the job? Which was the most fun? How would they improve on it another time? Group 4 needs to give the class a printed statement of how the money worked out. If you happened to end up with a profit, the class would need to decide on an appropriate charity connected with the faith community to which the money can be donated.

4   Arrange a questionnaire or a survey to go to each class in the school that attended, to see what they liked and didn't like about the party. Plan your questions carefully so that you get useful responses rather than just 'yes' or 'no'.

5   Write a report on the party for the school magazine, and another one for the local newspaper. Have you any suitable photographs you could include?

- List the three most important things you look for when shopping for clothes.

- Do you ever check the label? What do you look for?

- Does it matter where the clothes were made? Why?

- 'Paying as little as you can is the most important thing.' Give the arguments for and against this statement. Which side are you on?

Size 12

Made in Haiti
50% Cotton
50% Polyester
100% Sweatshop labour
14-hour shifts, 7 days a week
28 cents per hour

No right to speak

4.1 Sweat shop

An American clothes producer who runs this sweat shop said: 'We have a factory in China where we have 250 people. We own them; it's our factory. We pay them £23.60 a month and they work 28 days a month. They work from 7 am to 11 pm with two breaks for lunch and dinner. They all sleep together; 16 people to a room stacked on four bunks to a corner. Generally, they're young girls that come from the hills.' (CAFOD website)

- Are there any aspects of the owner's comments that you think are wrong?

- Why do you think he can always find people to work in his factory?

- Should he change the working conditions to the same as those in America?

- What would the effect of that be on us? Do you think that is acceptable?

Did you know?

- Bangladesh is Europe's largest supplier of T-shirts. Some workers there earn 65p for a 12-hour day.

- 99% of branded trainers are made in Asia where wages range from 23p to 46p an hour.

- 120 million children aged 5–14 work full-time.

- Garment workers in Mexico produce 70% more than their US counterparts for 10% of the wage bill.

- Which of these facts do you think we should be most concerned about? Why?

- Do you think it is our business to get involved with what happens in another country? Why?

36

IT'S TIME FOR JUSTICE

CAFOD

CAFOD is the Catholic Fund for Overseas Development. They are very concerned about clothes production and have conducted many surveys and written reports about what is going on.

> We believe that all human beings have a right to dignity and respect and that the world's resources are a gift to be shared by all men and women, whatever their race, nationality or religion. (*CAFOD*)

> The Church insists that an employed person is a full human being, not a commodity to be bought and sold according to market requirements. Workers have rights which Catholic teaching has consistently maintained are superior to those of capital. These include the right to decent work, to just wages, to security of employment, to adequate rest and holidays, to limitation of hours of work, to health and safety measures, to non-discrimination, the right to form and join trade unions, and, as a last resort, to go on strike. (*Statement by the Catholic Bishops, 1996*)

- What is meant by 'workers have rights which … are superior to capital'? Would everyone connected with a company agree with that? Why?

- Look at CAFOD's website and read their report on the Asian garment industry. Use their evidence, along with any more you can find, to write a magazine article that will make shoppers aware of the situation.

- Role-play a conversation between a CAFOD researcher and someone shopping for a pair of jeans.

- Do you think religious people should get involved in the way businesses are run? Why?

ETI

A few years ago CAFOD and Christian Aid joined with retail companies and the International Trade Union Movement to set up the Ethical Trading Initiative. They concentrated their work in three production areas initially: garments in China, wine in South Africa, and horticulture in Zimbabwe. Look at their website and report back to the group on the progress that has been made.

Jeans

Maria stitches jeans for a living. She works in a factory on the Mexican/US border which employs thousands of Mexican migrant workers. Maria lives in a tiny room, which is home to herself and eight other garment workers. The shanty town that has grown up around the factory has no electricity, running water or sewerage system.

Maria's shift starts at 8.30 am and lasts 12 hours. If she does not finish her set production goals she must work later without pay. Maria works through Saturdays from 8 am to 5 pm without a lunch break. She earns between 30 and 50 US dollars a week. Her fellow workers may be as young as 12 or 13 years old.

Workers are searched when they leave for lunch and at the end of the day to check that they aren't stealing materials. Women are given urine tests, and if they are found to be pregnant they are fired. Arriving 15 minutes late costs three days' work without pay.

- Look up the current exchange rate and calculate Maria's wages. What sort of wage would you expect someone in the UK to earn for doing that job?

- Look at page 78 to see if any of Maria's human rights are being abused.

Levi Strauss jeans are sold all over the world. Everybody wants good-quality jeans at the cheapest possible price. Salaries have risen so much in the USA that Levi Strauss have had to look abroad for production. Wages are considerably lower in some developing countries, but that might be because people work in poor conditions. Conditions like those described on pages 36 and 38 are of concern to the company.

There was public outcry in America in 1992 when a newspaper revealed that Levi Strauss jeans were being made by Chinese prisoners. The company reacted immediately and was the first multinational company to develop rules for the way workers making their garments must be treated.

- Workers must have healthy, safe working conditions.
- Workers must be treated with dignity and respect.

In 1993 Levi Strauss stopped their production in Myanmar (Burma), saying, 'Under current circumstances, it is not possible to do business in Myanmar without directly supporting the military government and its pervasive violation of human rights.'

Find out more about Levi Strauss on their website.

1   What are their four core values? Which of these could have any connection with the way their products are made?

2   Why do they think it makes good business sense to have values like this?

3   With a partner, list the problems and the benefits of moving the manufacture of clothes to a developing country. Give a 5-minute presentation to the group on this.

4   Why might people object to Chinese prisoners making jeans?

Over to you

You work for a company that makes designer unisex cotton T-shirts. You have been asked to investigate having the garments cut and stitched in a developing country that has a much lower standard of living than the UK.

What sort of treatment are you going to insist on for the workers? With a partner, go through these key areas and set up your code of conduct.

1 **Forced labour** – Will you accept the use of prisoners as workers?

2 **Child labour** – Is this acceptable? What minimum age? Should they receive any education? Rate of pay?

3 **Harassment and abuse at work** – What rules will you lay down for the employer?

4 **Discrimination** – What rules will you lay down about this area? Is the factory obliged to employ anybody?

5 **Health and safety** – What minimum hygiene and safety standards will you insist on in the factory? What will happen to employees who suffer an accident at work?

6 **Hours of work** – What will be the maximum working week? Will you permit overtime? Will it be voluntary? Will it be paid? What breaks are permitted in a day? Will there be any paid holiday entitlement?

7 **Wages** – How will the factory decide on the right money for the job?

8 **Trade unions** – Will you allow the workers the right to bargain over wages individually or in a group?

- You could look at CAFOD's Ethical Trading Initiative base code on their website to see their suggestions in this area.

- Remember: you have to be fair to the people who make your clothes *and* be fair to the company's shareholders. If the T-shirts are too expensive, they won't sell, the share-holders will pull out and your firm will go bust. That will put all the workers in the developing world out of a job too. How far are you prepared to compromise your principles?

Design and market your own product

Well done! You have succeeded in getting a good product at a fair price. Nobody is getting ripped off. Your company should do well, but people need to know that they are buying your product and not that of someone else who may have lower standards.

In groups of three or four

1   Design a label to go on all the clothes made by your company to show that they are ethically traded.

2   What sort of simple logo could your labels and advertising carry to show that this is a product made by people who are fairly treated?

3   Some customers want to show that they are supporting an ethical product. Create several suitable designs to go on the front of T-shirts.

4   Write a press release that might be sent to newspapers and radio stations explaining why your garments are more fairly produced than some others you could name – and you can name them if you have evidence to support your remarks!

5   There has been much bad publicity about the use of pesticides on cotton. It is claimed that cotton production uses a higher volume of toxic pesticides than any other crop, causing a million cases of human poisoning every year. Investigate this situation. Greenpeace or Friends of the Earth may be able to help you. You will need to reassure your customers that you are aware of this problem and have taken appropriate action.

6   Don't forget your shareholders. Without them your company will not be able to operate. Write a letter to them explaining why it makes good business sense to trade ethically.

7   You could look at the bad publicity some manufacturers of leading brands of trainers receive on the internet, as evidence that consumers do care about the way their goods are produced.

Unit 4 *feedback*

Groupwork

1 In groups of three or four, organise a campaign to raise awareness amongst pupils in the lower school about the way some clothes are made. You will need a snappy name for your campaign. Make some posters to highlight the problem. You will also need to tell pupils how they can check on the clothes they are buying and which designer labels treat their employees fairly.

2 Look at CAFOD's website and read the data they have compiled on individual companies. Which company seems most concerned about ethical trading? Who comes out worst, and why? You could email one of the companies that came out badly to ask them what they are doing about this issue.

3 Did you know anything about the way garments were produced before you read this unit? Will it change the way you buy in the future? Why?

4 Look at the website of Sweatshop Watch and the Ethical Trading Initiative. Make a list of full British members so that you know what you are buying in the future.

5 Imagine your agency has just landed a big contract with one of the country's leading supermarket chains. They sell food, clothes, electrical goods, etc. Because there has been a lot of publicity about ethical trading, the supermarket wants you to sort things out for them. The staff in the store need to know about ethical trading in case customers ask about it. Prepare an A5 sheet that will fit into the envelope with their monthly payslip. Tell them what ethical trading means. Explain why the company is concerned and what it is doing about it.

6 Choose three major clothes producers, whose fashions you like, to discover their company policy on the use of sweatshops. You could email them directly with your questions if their website is not specific enough. Make a spreadsheet to compare the results.

Getting tough on crime

- 12 is the youngest age for tagging.

- Around 70,000 people are in UK prisons.

- 3% of young people are responsible for 25% of crime.

- The UK locks up more teenagers than most European countries.

- 10 is the age a person is responsible for their actions under the criminal law in the UK.

- 78% of young people in trouble with the law have been permanently excluded from school.

- Around 3,270 people of all ages are currently tagged in the UK.

- 1,800 12–18 year-olds are expected to be tagged every year.

Find out how tagging works. Why is it being used?

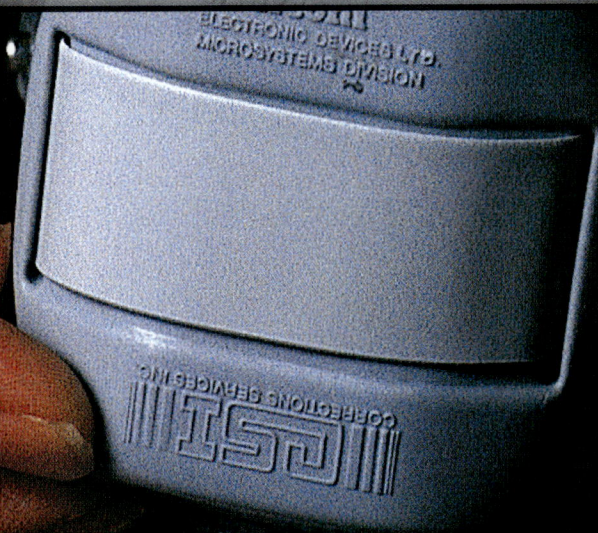

5.1 Car crime

- With a partner list the four crimes you think are the worst and explain why.

- How seriously would you rate car crime versus other crimes? Is it mainly something kids do and grow out of?

> **Recent research among people convicted of a car crime**
>
> **75%** had been convicted of a mainstream offence before.
>
> **73%** tested positive for cannabis.
>
> **36%** tested positive for alcohol.
>
> **97%** were male.
>
> **33%** were under 18.
>
> **30%** were aged 18–21.
>
> **44%** were convicted of another car theft within a year.
>
> **1 in 5** crimes is connected with a vehicle.

- Study the data above. Write a short profile of the type of person most likely to be involved in some type of car crime.

- Why do you think that is?

The victims

People get very upset if they are the victim of a crime. Indeed, the stress it causes can often be worse than the loss. Research shows that 83% of people were badly shaken when their car was stolen and 46% of them suffered severe stress.

- Why do you think it caused so much stress even though the car was insured?

People aged 18–29 worry most about having their car stolen.

- Why do you think that is? Think about the sorts of places they go to, the company they keep, the cost of the car to them, etc.

- List all the problems a person might suffer if their car was stolen.

44

Kid from hell!

An 11-year-old boy, who could not be named for legal reasons, appeared at Cardiff Youth Court today. Locals call him 'the kid from hell' and say he is a 'one-person crime wave' because he steals so many cars. The court was told the boy had committed 'an appalling catalogue of offences during a spree of car thefts' over two years. On average he stole one car every day and drove them even though he was only 4 ft 6 inches tall. His most recent offence involved stealing and driving a van at 70 mph even though he was so short he had to prop himself up in order to reach the pedals.

Although he has admitted to more than 20 motoring offences, the court has no powers to detain him until he reaches his twelfth birthday. Attempts to impose a 13-hour curfew on the child have failed to stop him re-offending.

What do you think?

In groups of three or four, discuss this real-life case and share your thoughts with the class.

1   If you were at the Cardiff Youth Court, what would you recommend they did with the boy on this occasion? What would be the purpose of this action?

2   How much would you hold his parents responsible for his behaviour?

3   How responsible should a child of that age be for his behaviour? Does his school have any responsibility?

4   What do you think has caused this situation?

5   Look at the Government's Crime Reduction website. When and where is car crime most likely to take place?

Tackling the causes of crime

With a partner

List at least six things you think cause crime.

1   Would you consider any of these a reason to treat the criminal more leniently? Why?

2   Would you like to see a fixed punishment for every crime or should each case be judged individually? Why?

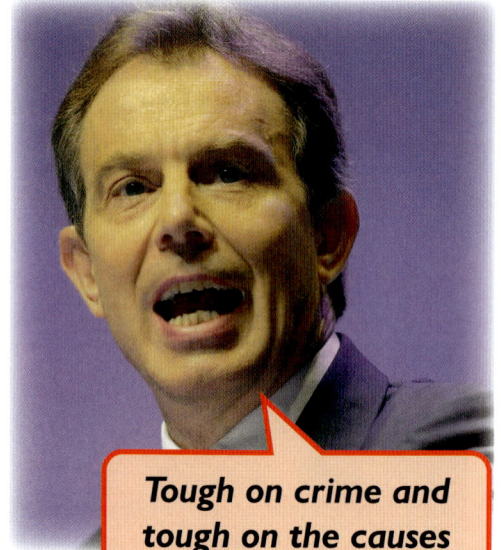

> *Tough on crime and tough on the causes of crime*

> Islam says that alcohol and drugs cause many problems because they act on the brain making people lose control and act in a stupid way. That might just result in silly behaviour but it could also lead to quarrels, fights and crime. The Qur'an is clear that no Muslim should drink alcohol.

> 'They ask you about drinking and gambling. Say: "There is great harm in both, although they have some benefit for men; but their harm is far greater than their benefits." ' (*Qur'an 2:19*)

● Do you think many crimes committed in your area are connected with alcohol or drug abuse? Is it because people are under the influence of drink or drugs, or want money to buy them? What could be done to tackle this problem?

A Christian response to crime

On the opposite page is an account of the work of a Christian charity. Look at The Children's Society's website for more details about their work on Youth Justice.

Discuss with a partner what you feel about religious groups getting involved in this sort of thing. What advantages could there be? What disadvantages?

The Children's Society is the fourth largest children's charity in Britain.

In over a hundred projects all over England and Wales, we're working to develop long-term solutions to the very serious problems faced by some of the country's most vulnerable children and young people every day.

Founded in 1881 by Edward Rudolf, who responded to children in need out of his own deep Christian convictions, the Society continues to have close links with the Church of England and the Church in Wales.

Youth Justice – our response

Youth crime is the subject of heated debate. Crime has an impact on everyone's life: the victim, the young person who has been charged, their families, the community. Finding a balance between the fair treatment of children and young people who come before the courts and effective responses to youth crime is a difficult task. The Children's Society wishes to reduce the risk of children and young people becoming involved in crime and works with those who do become involved to help them lead responsible, law-abiding lives.

Too many young people are involved in crime, as victims and offenders, but they are also dealt with very harshly by the criminal justice system, in ways that are often ineffective and expensive. Increasing numbers of children and young people are being locked up, often in highly unsuitable conditions.

A third of the prison population has been in care as a child, one in four of young people in trouble have been excluded from school, half of young remand prisoners have mental health problems. These issues need to be addressed in ways that are just and humane if we are serious about wanting to reduce the risk of offending.

Jane's Story

Jane, aged 16, made a distraught telephone call to The Children's Society after being charged with robbery. She told us her 'boyfriend' was putting her under pressure and bullying her into stealing. During an initial meeting with Jane and her parents, it emerged she was trapped in a damaging relationship from which she felt unable to escape. The fact that she lived with her boyfriend compounded the problem, as he was pressurising her to re-offend while on bail. This would almost certainly have resulted in her being remanded to prison.

As part of a bail support programme, the staff at The Children's Society were able to find Jane alternative supported accommodation to remove her from the immediate pressure she was under. Jane got through her bail successfully and did not receive a prison sentence. Thanks to our project's help with benefits and health and emotional problems, Jane is now living independently and has not committed any further offences.

5.3 What is a just punishment?

Read the following case studies.

A Steve and Darren were larking around on the street. They noticed that a smart black holdall had been left on the front seat of one car, so they smashed the window, grabbed the bag and ran off. The bag contained nappies and a baby's changing things. It was valued at £25. The lads threw it over a hedge, keeping none of the contents.

B Paul had been drinking with his girlfriend Vicky and they had both had too much to drink. Walking home they passed a petrol station. Vicky dared Paul to jump into the blue Honda that had been left with its keys in the ignition as the driver was paying for petrol. The couple drove off in the car.

C Dave was walking by the flats when he saw a car outside with the label 'Doctor on call' on the windscreen. Believing that all doctors carry drugs, he smashed the side window, got in and drove off. There was nothing in the car so he dumped it in a factory carpark and torched it.

With a partner

In these instances the criminals were caught. What sentence would you like to see passed on each of the people named? Why? To teach them a lesson? To warn off others? To make them suffer for what they have done? To make the victim feel better? To make everybody feel safer? Or is there another reason? Is there anything you think should be done for the victims of these crimes?

What do Christians think about crime?

The Ten Commandments, which were set down well over two thousand years ago, include strict rules for Jews and Christians that clearly state: 'You must not steal' and 'You must not murder'. People who commit such crimes are punished. The Christian religion is also concerned that a criminal understands what they have done wrong and doesn't do it again. Most Christians would see this as a victory for everyone, and in keeping with Jesus' teaching about repentance and forgiveness.

Jesus made it plain that he was concerned about all people, even criminals.

> People who are well do not need a doctor, but only those who are sick. I have not come to call respectable people, but outcasts. *(Mark 2:17)*

He told many stories about people who had done wrong and were forgiven, but in most cases they had to make the first move.

- Read the parable of the Lost Son in Luke 15:11–32.

- What do you think the long-term effect of the father's treatment would be on the younger boy?

- How could the father have treated him differently? What effect would that have had?

Some Christians choose to work for organisations like The Children's Society – see page 47. Their aim is to put Jesus' message of love, like that in the parable of the Lost Son, into action. Other Christians work to tackle the causes of crime, which they believe arise from things like poverty or poor housing conditions.

All prisons have a chaplain attached to them. Find out what the job involves. Research Elizabeth Fry, a famous prison visitor in the early 19th century. How is her work continued today by the Quakers? What is the point of it?

Unit 5 feedback

1 Research and produce a poster-sized diagram to show how the legal system deals with a young offender aged 16 from the moment they are arrested.

2 Role-play an interview between one of the characters in the case studies on page 48 and a Year 12 student who is saving up to buy a car.

3 Mobile phone theft worries many young people. Use the internet to read some recent newspaper articles and find some statistics. Write a magazine article advising people on how to avoid it happening to them. Mention the stress it causes victims. Or display the essence of the article as a poster that can be put up around the school to warn everyone.

4 Use the internet to investigate projects like 'UK Motor Projects' which uses cars, motorbikes and driving as a basis for reforming young offenders. Report back on what they do, and on their success rate.

5 Investigate the possibility of inviting an outside speaker to talk to the group about Youth Justice.

Groupwork

6 Devise a survey that you could conduct in school and amongst family and friends. The aim is to find out about the fear of crime in your area.

- Use ICT to create the survey. It will need a column to record the age group. You will also need to record the type of crime that worries them most.

- Compare your findings with the reality. Use the Home Office website for crime statistics.

- What conclusions do you reach about people's fear of crime?

What's your agenda?

The Earth Summit at Rio

The United Nations met at Rio de Janeiro in 1992 to discuss what we are doing to the planet. This was the first time so many nations had got together to talk about environmental issues. The important thing to come out of the summit was that governments accepted the fact that the solution lay in their hands. As a result, an agenda, or plan of action, was drawn up for the 21st century, and called Agenda 21. Ten years later the nations met again in South Africa to see what progress they had made.

• Look up the meaning of 'sustainable development'. Why does it matter?

6.1 Recognise this?

Planet Earth is 4,600,000,000 years old. If we condense this inconceivable time-span into something we can understand, then the Earth is like a person aged 46. Nothing is known about the first 7 years of this person's life, and only bits and pieces of information exist about the middle span, but we know that at the age of 42 the Earth began to flower. Dinosaurs and the great reptiles did not appear until one year ago, and in the middle of last week, man-like apes evolved into ape-like men and at the weekend, the last ice age enveloped the Earth.

Modern man has been around for 4 hours. During the last hour Man discovered agriculture. The industrial revolution began a minute ago. During those sixty seconds of biological time, modern man has made a rubbish tip of a paradise. He has multiplied his numbers to plague proportions, caused the extinction of countless species of animals, ransacked the planet for fuels and now stands, like a brutish infant, gloating over his speedy take-over, on the brink of a war to end all wars and of effectively destroying this oasis of life in the solar system.

(Adapted from a piece by Greenpeace)

Do you think this is a fair description of what humans have been up to on the planet? Why?

- Make a list of the damage mentioned here that humans have caused.
- Add four more things you can think of to the list.
- Design your own cartoon to illustrate the idea of humans as the destroyers of the planet.

The solution?

Earth Summit

Sustainable development is about ensuring a better quality of life for everyone, both now and for generations to come.

Agenda 21

'Agenda 21 is a comprehensive plan of action to be taken globally, nationally and locally … in every area in which humans impact on the environment.' (UN website)

Local Agenda 21

It was agreed at the World Summit that talking was not enough. Every country must have its own agenda, or action plan, that would improve its use, and reduce its abuse, of the environment. If things were really to happen this must go right down to the grass-roots level. Every local area in a country must have its own Local Agenda 21 which states what it is doing to develop a sustainable environment. Included in this are businesses, schools, religious and community groups – basically, everybody.

- Look up the results of the World Summit on Sustainable Development in Johannesburg, South Africa, in 2002. This meeting looked at the progress that had been made since Rio. What areas had improved, and what actually got worse? What conclusions were reached?

- Look at the contents of Agenda 21 on the United Nations website. Make two columns in your exercise book or on a spreadsheet. In one column list the topics that have no connection with the UK. In the other column list the topics we should be concerned about in this country. Keep your lists to review later.

- Make contact with your local authority and ask them to send details of their Local Agenda 21. You could arrange for the officer in charge to come and tell the class what is going on and what the school can be doing as part of it.

- As a group, study the list of projects in your area's Local Agenda 21. Check on as many initiatives as you can, to see if progress is being made.

- Make some constructive suggestions to improve your local authority's performance. One area you might like to consider is waste management, which is mentioned on page 11. Do you think enough is being done in your area?

What do they say? And what do they do?

Christians believe that the world was created by God and continues to be sustained by God. Humans have been given responsibility to care for the world and look after it in a way that safeguards it for the future. (*Church of England*)

- Since Local Agenda 21 applies to church groups along with everyone else, find out from one local church how it is implementing the policy. Ask about areas that have been highlighted for action.

- Look at the website of the Christian Ecology Link to see what could be done towards Local Agenda 21.

The Earth we have been given is beautiful, bounteous and nourishing to the soul. It was perfectly clean when we got it, and we have a duty to return it to our children in this way. (*A Jewish response to the environment*)

- Look at the website of the Noah Project. This organisation takes its name from the story of Noah's ark: they say that when Noah took the animals into the ark two by two, he was 'preserving the earth's biodiversity'. What does that mean? Find out what the Noah Project's aims are. What connection could that have with Local Agenda 21?

Gandhi, probably the most influential Indian person ever, was a Hindu. He said: 'The world has enough for everyone's need, but not for everyone's greed.'

- What did he mean? Consult with your Geography department to learn why there are so many famines in Africa. Do you think there is any truth in Gandhi's statement?

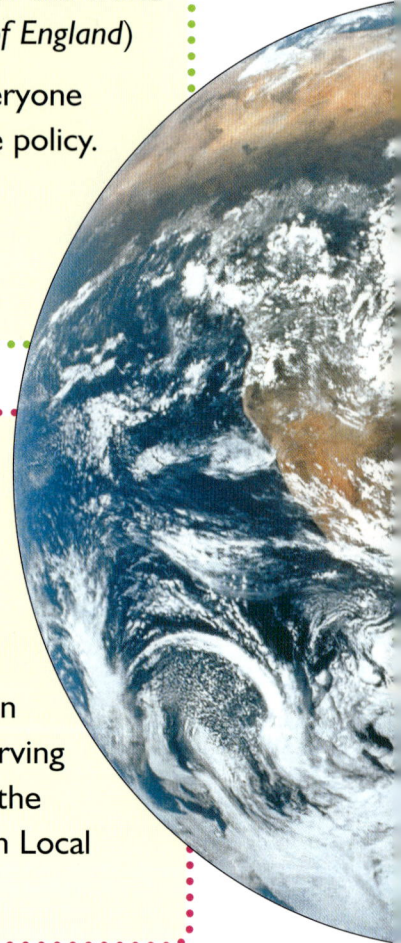

A Tibetan Buddhist monk says: 'I'm not an environmentalist, I'm not a botanist. I don't have any great deep knowledge about these things but I do feel very much part of planet earth. I feel the planet is like my mother and I would want to care for the planet as I would my mother, you know, and it works for me on that very simple level. I feel very upset when I see trees being decimated whatever part of the world it is. I think you can take from nature but you do it with respect.' (*Clear Vision*)

- Find out how these Tibetan monks live in an environmentally caring way on Holy Island off Arran in the west of Scotland.

Do you have to believe in God to care about the environment?

Humanists say: 'We should care about the future of our planet because we care about other human beings, even those not born yet. Because humanists have no belief in a god or supernatural force that will solve our problems for us, they know that human beings must take sole responsibility for sorting our environmental problems. We are the only ones capable of finding the solutions that can lead to a sustainable existence.' (*British Humanist Association*)

- Look at the British Humanist Association's website. Read in more detail about their environmental work. Which charities or organisations have their members taken an active part in?

Guru Nanak said: 'For the sake of posterity, those countless generations of unborn children to come, let us save this Earth.'

- Find out about the progress of the Sikh University dedicated to environmental studies, at Anandpur Sahib in the Punjab.

The Prophet Muhammad ﷺ said: 'The world is green and beautiful and God has appointed you his steward over it. The whole earth has been created as a place of worship pure and clean.'

- What do Muslims mean by 'stewardship'?

- Find out what the International Islamic University in Jordan is working to conserve.

Making a positive difference

'Before you finish eating your breakfast this morning you've depended on half the world. This is the way our universe is structured… We aren't going to have peace on earth until we recognise this basic fact.' (*Martin Luther King*)

With a partner

Test Martin Luther King's statement. Write down all the products you have used from the moment you got out of bed until you finished your breakfast – what you ate, wore, used. Try and work out what they were made of, where they were made and how they got to you. You may find it helpful to draw this as a spider diagram radiating out from you.

This is one of many farmers' markets, part of Local Agenda 21, in operation in Britain. This one is held once a month all year in Ludlow, Shropshire. Goods produced locally are brought here for sale and include fruit and vegetables, wine, organic bread, meat and dairy produce, honey and beeswax products and even locally crafted wooden toys. What is the advantage for the producer? What is the advantage for the consumer? Why might some producers and consumers prefer to deal with a supermarket chain? If you get the chance, compare the type, quality and price of goods offered for sale at a local market with those in a supermarket. What differences did you notice?

This is a solar-powered telephone box at CAT, the Centre for Alternative Technology. It is situated on a hill in Machynlleth in Wales and can be reached by a water-powered funicular railway. CAT is an environmental project set up in 1975 to find ways of living in harmony with the planet rather than destroying it. CAT's ideas were way ahead of Agenda 21.

CAT says:

'We demonstrate ways in which people, nature and technology can live together successfully. [It may not be easy but] if we want to survive into the future and have a relatively smooth ride our best bet lies with understanding and working with those natural processes, rather than trying to "conquer" nature.'

- CAT lists eight Global Enemies on its website. Divide the class into eight groups and each group take one enemy. Study it. Find out what is going on locally to improve things in this area. Report back to the class. Plan how you can make the school community aware of this issue and suggest ways they can assist. You could involve the Geography department.

- Take a virtual tour of CAT on their website. You can discover your own green rating using their '25 Ways to Save the Planet'.

- Investigate the different types of ecologically friendly houses that CAT has built, and report back to the group. Which did you think was the weirdest? How did it work?

Unit 6 *feedback*

1 The Local Government Act 2000 requires local authorities to consult with young people during policy- and decision-making. Contact your local authority and find out if, and how, they are putting this into operation. Find out what part of Local Agenda 21 they are currently working on, to make sure your voice is heard. Decide what message your class wants to send to them. Make sure they get the message!

2 Look back at the list you first made in response to the second task on page 53. Do you still agree with it? Are there any topics you would move to a different column now? Why? As a class compare your results and reasoning.

3 Find out what is involved in becoming an Eco-School as part of Local Agenda 21. Once you have listed the seven basic steps, design a questionnaire to find out pupils' views on the project before you take it forward. Report your findings to the school council.

4 Use the World Wildlife Fund's education website to get up-to-date information on the World Summit and details of an area in which you are especially interested.

5 Make a poster of 'Top 20 Tips to save the Earth'.

Debate

Organise a class debate on this motion:

> It is right to build a new road to improve traffic getting in and out of the town. This will cut down on traffic jams which cause pollution from car engines, waste business time and put stress on the drivers. It is worth destroying the habitat of many plants and animals to do this.

You will need people to represent each of the following to give their opinions:

- a motoring organisation
- the Wildlife Trust
- the local Chamber of Commerce
- local inhabitants.

I protest!

Rose Cottle, aged 102, took her protest to 10 Downing Street in March 2002. She delivered a petition with more than 5,000 signatures to the Prime Minister, protesting about the closure of the care-home she lives in. Property prices had risen so much that the owners of the home decided to sell the site for development. It is the second time in three years that this elderly lady has been turned out of her home. 'This sort of thing should not be happening to people in their nineties and hundreds,' she said. 'These old people are only going to clog up hospitals if there aren't enough rooms for us.'

- Why do people collect signatures on a petition?
- Do you think this was the most effective way of protesting about the home being closed? Why?
- Rose Cottle's protest made the national papers, the TV and radio news. Why?

7.1 What right do I have to protest?

Anything? Anywhere? Any time?

Check the full version of the 1998 UK Human Rights Act on the internet to find out whether you are free to think what you like, to say what you like, to stand up in public. Are you?

The importance of being heard

Everyone has a right to make their views known. One person famously said, 'I don't agree with your views but I will defend to the death your right to hold them.' Why would anyone die for somebody else's opinion if they don't agree with it? Try guessing when that statement was made. (The answer is on page 66, but have a guess first!)

The importance of young people's voices

The United Nations recognises that children and young people not only have a right to be heard, but that they have something to say which the world should listen to. A Special Session in which children and young people took part was held in May 2002. Use the internet to discover what they discussed and who attended the Session.

> The child shall have the right to freedom of expression; this right shall include freedom to seek, receive and impart information and ideas of all kinds, regardless of frontiers, either orally, in writing or in print, in the form of art, or through any other media of the child's choice.
>
> *Convention on the Rights of the Child, Article 13:1*

- What have children got to say that is worth listening to?

60

What difference can I make?

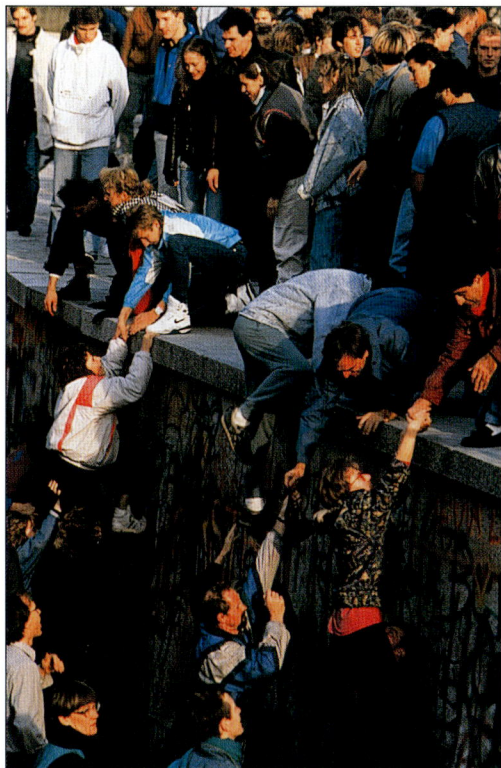

It was the power of the people in the end that demolished the Berlin Wall in 1989. This wall was built in 1961 to prevent people from fleeing the Communist area of the German city. Over the years, hundreds of people were killed by Communist border guards as they tried to flee to the West. Find out how, after 28 years, the wall came down without bloodshed.

It is so easy to believe that we are insignificant, that we can't have any effect on things, but here are a few other people's remarks on the subject:

- If you think you're too small to be effective, you've obviously never been in bed with a mosquito! (*Anon*)

- It is not the kings and generals that make history, but the masses of the people. (*Nelson Mandela*)

- To avoid criticism, don't do anything, say anything or be anything. (*Anon*)

- You can make a difference. You can press the governments of the world to do more. (*Gordon Brown, UK Chancellor of the Exchequer*)

- Never doubt that a small group of thoughtful committed citizens can change the world; indeed it's the only thing that ever has. (*Margaret Mead*)

- Take one of these quotations and explain in your own words what the person is saying. What evidence could you put forward to support their view? What seems to contradict it? How powerful do you think your voice could be?

61

Should Christians get involved?

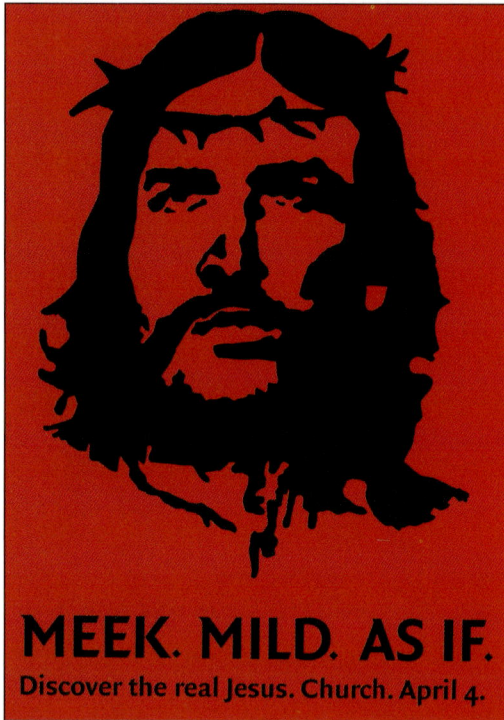

MEEK. MILD. AS IF.
Discover the real Jesus. Church. April 4.

This poster was designed to portray Jesus as a radical leader who was quite prepared to fight against the injustices of his day. Indeed it was said the artist based this picture of Jesus on the face of the famous freedom-fighter Che Guevara. Some Christians were upset by this. Research the life of Che Guevara to find out why some Christians might be upset about this association. If you are able to find a picture of the freedom-fighter, compare it with this poster.

Christians look to the life and teachings of Jesus for guidance on whether they should get involved in campaigning. The scriptures leave them in no doubt that Jesus thought people should stand up for what they believe in. He paid the ultimate price for his beliefs by giving his life.

The problem Christians face is deciding exactly how Jesus intended them to protest against injustice.

> On the one hand Jesus said, 'Do not think that I have come to bring peace to the world. No, I did not come to bring peace, but a sword. Whoever does not take up his cross and follow in my steps is not fit to be my disciple.' (*Matthew 10:34, 38*)

> Yet he also said: 'Do not take revenge on someone who wrongs you. If anyone slaps you on the right cheek, let him slap your left cheek too.' (*Matthew 5:39*)

- Do these two quotations contradict each other? Are they talking about the same things, or different ones?

An anti-nuclear protester is led away by police officers after demonstrators blocked the entrance to the Faslane nuclear base on Valentine's Day 2000.

- What effect do you think these people will have on government policy? How else could they make their voice heard? Do you think they should?

Non-violent protest

Many people believe in protesting in a non-violent way, like taking part in marches through the street, or big rallies in Trafalgar Square, or something similar to the protest in the picture. Martin Luther King, like the great Hindu leader Gandhi, made use of civil disobedience which included refusing to pay taxes or to buy goods from a certain country, or simply making a public nuisance of themselves.

- Do you think this is an acceptable way to make your point? Although non-violent, some of these tactics are illegal. What are the advantages and disadvantages of this sort of protest?

Find out about ...

- Archbishop Tutu's campaign (see page 73). Why did he do it?

- Gandhi's campaign to boycott everything British when he was working towards Indian independence. Did it work? Why?

- Camillo Torres, a Roman Catholic priest, who said, 'I believe the revolutionary struggle is appropriate for the Christian,' and joined the guerrilla army in Colombia. What happened to him?

7.3 Campaigning

Here are some issues you might like to consider that have been in the news recently: cloning, torture, a specific environmental problem, abortion, euthanasia, equal rights, or another topic that has been in the news or mentioned in this book.

In groups of three or four

Choose an ethical issue to focus on.

1 Research it. The internet is an excellent place to start.

2 Find out which organisations are concerned about this issue and what they are doing.

3 Get facts and figures about the case.

4 Work out a reasoned argument why people should be concerned about your issue.

Either ...

Make a study of the campaign around this issue.

1 Find the earliest references you can to the start of the campaign. You could email the organisation(s) currently involved to ask about its early history.

2 Find out how the movement has grown. Is it of local, national or international interest?

3 Create a diagram to show how the campaign has widened its appeal.

4 Make a list of all the methods of campaigning or protesting that have been used. Try to find out which were the most successful.

5 Study some newspaper reports of this campaign to see how it has been reported. Has it generated any negative publicity? If so, why?

6 What have been the high points of the campaign so far?

Do you think people should have the right to march in support of their views? Why? What problems might it cause?

Or ...

Get involved yourselves. Your aim will be to make other people aware of the issue that concerns you, to make them think more deeply about it and perhaps to give their support. There are many things you could do to spread the message beyond yourself – you could start within the class, move into the school and perhaps take your concern out to the wider community.

Before you start to move outside your small group you need to be sure of your facts. Check and double-check your research. The internet is likely to give you the most up-to-date information and will provide you with contacts with other groups, but remember that anybody can put anything on a website – it isn't always true. It would be a good idea to make contact with a reputable organisation, tell them what you are doing and ask for more detailed information.

When you have established the current situation, decide what you can realistically hope to achieve.

Which of the following are going to be the most effective ways of achieving your aims? For each one, think what it could do for your campaign, and how you can set about it.

- Write to your MP.
- Write to a local and national paper.
- Try to get a slot on local radio to put your point of view.
- Inform and involve your school.
- Make a video.

- Post information on the school's website.
- Produce a poster and a handout.
- Produce a press release.
- Issue a regular newsletter/bulletin and/or email people with updates.

Unit 7 feedback

1   If you actively pursued a campaign, evaluate its success. Look back at your aim and as a group decide how far you succeeded. What is the evidence of that? Do you think the amount of work you all put into it was enough/enjoyable/a wasted effort?

2   Research the life and death of Oscar Romero. Write a newspaper report of his death. Decide whether you are writing for a rebel newspaper or a government one. Would it make any difference?

3   What does this logo symbolise? Investigate this campaign from its earliest days to the present, and produce a flow chart to show its progress. Why did some Christian priests get involved?

4   The quotation on page 60 came from Voltaire, a famous philosopher and activist who lived in France in the 18th century at the time of the French Revolution. You might like to find out more about him.

Discussion

If everyone has the right to be heard, would you allow the following groups to hold public meetings? What are your reasons?

* Those who want the freedom to walk around the streets naked.

* Those who support the use of force to stop animals appearing in circuses.

* Those who want a change in the law to allow paedophiles to operate freely.

* Those who want houses in the town to be sold or rented only to people who were born in the town.

You're different

- What do you think of this Christian picture?

- What race is Jesus likely to have been?

- So what sort of colouring is he likely to have had?

- Why do people make him look as they do – white, fair-haired, European …?

- Does that matter?

8.1 You're racist

> You're racist!

> So. What's wrong with that? You're sexist!

What do people mean when they say someone is racist? Are the speech bubbles coming from the people you would expect?

Do you think sexism is as harmful as racism? Why?

With a partner

1   Role-play the scene above. You will need to start before the incident in the picture and carry it beyond to show the outcome.

2   Should this be treated as just a squabble between two people? Decide whether it is better to intervene or to leave the situation alone. If this was happening in school, what would you recommend the year head to do?

3   Do you think the media has any impact on scenes like this one? Discuss incidents of racism you have seen on TV programmes. Were there any instances where racism was made out to be a bad thing or as something that was justified?

4   What is the worst thing that could come from a verbal exchange like this one?

On 22 April 1993 Stephen Lawrence was stabbed to death in a street in south-east London. He was an ordinary, hard-working 18-year-old student in Year 13 who had never been in trouble. It is believed that a group of white youths killed him simply because he was black. People heard them shouting racist abuse at Stephen shortly before he was stabbed.

The murder of their son was bad enough for Stephen's parents to suffer, but it was made worse by the way the police treated them. The Lawrence family felt the police did not bother to find the killers because Stephen was black, despite the fact that the names of five suspects came up early on. In the end the Lawrences had to bring a private prosecution against three of those suspects. Even then the family found their efforts thwarted when a judge ruled that one eye-witness's evidence was unreliable. Mrs Lawrence said, 'We will never know if we had enough evidence or not, because the jury were never given the opportunity to make that judgement. The judge directed them to return a verdict of not guilty.' Under British law, a person cannot be tried again for the same crime, no matter what new evidence might be uncovered.

The Lawrence family feel let down by the British authorities simply because they are black. They have since campaigned to have Stephen's case thoroughly investigated to find out what went wrong and to prevent others from minority groups suffering similar treatment.

The Macpherson Inquiry investigated all aspects of the Stephen Lawrence case and concluded there was 'institutional racism' in the police force. Seventy changes were recommended in lots of areas from law to education to try and prevent such a case re-occurring.

- Someone said: 'Stephen Lawrence died because people around him refused to see a person.' What *did* people see? What is the difference?

- Use the website of a national newspaper (like *The Guardian*) to discover more details about this case. Give five reasons why the Stephen Lawrence case has been called 'a milestone in race relations'. Name two things the Macpherson Report recommended. Has anything changed as a result of Stephen's death?

8.2 What do the world religions say about racism and discrimination?

Without exception all world religions condemn racism and prejudice because they believe everyone was made the same. Those religions that believe in a God (Buddhism does not) say that if God made everything and everybody, then to treat some people as inferior is the same as criticising God.

Christianity says:

> So there is no difference between Jews and Gentiles, between slaves and free men, between men and women; you are all one in union with Christ Jesus. (*Galatians 3:28*)

This was the advice St Paul gave to the new Christian community in Galatia. (Gentiles are non-Jews.)

There are several incidents in Jesus' life and in stories he told that show he believed everyone was of equal worth in his eyes and in the eyes of God.

- Look at the story of the Good Samaritan in Luke 10:25–37. What part of this story is to do with racism?

Sikhism says:

The tenth guru, Guru Gobind Singh, told his followers:

> Though they use different dresses according to the influence of regional customs, all people have the same eyes, ears, body and figure made out of the compounds of earth, air, fire and water.

- How are these teachings about equality put into practice in the gurdwara?

Islam says:

> All people are equal like the teeth of a comb. No Arab can claim merit over a non-Arab, nor a white over a black person, nor a male over a female. (*The Hadith*)

- A Muslim would say Hajj was a perfect example of Muslims refusing to be racist. Why?

Hinduism says:

> In mankind, nobody is higher or lower nor is anybody of middle status. Everybody with concerted effort toils along the path of progress. (*Rig Veda 5-59-6*)

Buddhism says:

The Buddha taught respect for all living beings irrespective of race. Geshe Kelsang, a modern Buddhist teacher, said:

> If we think of all the living beings as one body, one in wishing to be free from suffering, we will not hesitate to alleviate their suffering.

Judaism says:

> Do not ill-treat foreigners who are living in your land. Treat them as you would a fellow-Israelite, and love them as you love yourselves. Remember that you were once a foreigner in the land of Egypt. (*Leviticus 19:33–34*)

- What incident is the Leviticus quotation referring to? How were the Jews treated then?

Do you need to know what I look like before you decide how to treat me?

8.3 Fighting racism

These people are fighting racial issues. The year 2001 witnessed some of the worst racial riots Britain has ever seen. Both sides accused the other of inciting racial hatred and they fought it out on the streets. Who won? Nobody. The area they live in is now in a worse state than it was beforehand. Buildings were damaged. Each side distrusts the other and nobody feels safe walking down the street on their own. Is this the best way to fight racism?

Martin Luther King said:

> I have a dream that my four little children will one day live in a nation where they will not be judged by the colour of their skin, but by the sort of persons they are. I have a dream that one day … all God's children, black, white, Jews and Gentiles, Protestants and Catholics, will be able to join hands and sing in the words of the black people's old song, 'Free at last, free at last, thank God Almighty, we are free at last!'

Martin Luther King believed that peaceful protest was the key to making lasting change. He led marches and protests to draw attention to the strength of people's feelings. His campaign was based on civil disobedience. That means refusing to do things the authorities wanted, rather than using violence.

- Find out what the bus boycott was and why it was so successful.

- Why does civil disobedience cause authorities more problems than violence?

Archbishop Desmond Tutu said:

> If the only thing that we ever did was to say strongly to people, please stop the violence, we will have advanced the kingdom of God in an incredible way.

Archbishop Tutu worked to gain equal rights for blacks and whites in South Africa. He believes peaceful methods are the best way to draw attention to injustices. In one famous incident in 1989, he led a group of supporters onto a whites-only beach in South Africa. Because he was black and so were many of his supporters, they were all chased off the beach by the police with whips. People were outraged. Publicity like this did more to create change than any riot would have done. It helped achieve the election of the country's first black president, Nelson Mandela, in 1994.

In 2002, Halle Berry was awarded an Oscar for her role in the film 'Monster's Ball'. She responded with an emotional speech about racism. 'It's been 74 years! 74 years from the first Oscar night until a black woman won the award for best actress.' She said, 'This moment is so much bigger than me… It is for every nameless, faceless woman of colour who now has a chance because this door tonight has been opened.'

With a partner

1   Write down possible reasons why no black women had won this award before (for example, 'There are no black actresses'). Then go through your list and decide which you think is most likely.

2   Try to find out when the first black man won an Oscar.

3   Do you think there is racism in such situations? Why?

8.4 Is football racist?

- Would you say that was racism? Why?

Research undertaken by Sheffield Hallam University showed that only a small percentage of people from ethnic minorities attended matches but that racist incidents increased dramatically in the area around football grounds on match days. This led to the formation of a partnership between football fans, Sheffield United Football Club, the local council, youth and community groups, schools, the church, police and the Commission for Racial Equality.

'Football Unites, Racism Divides' (FURD) believes that football, as the world's most popular game, can help to bring people together – people from different backgrounds – to play, watch and enjoy the game, and to break down barriers created by ignorance or prejudice.

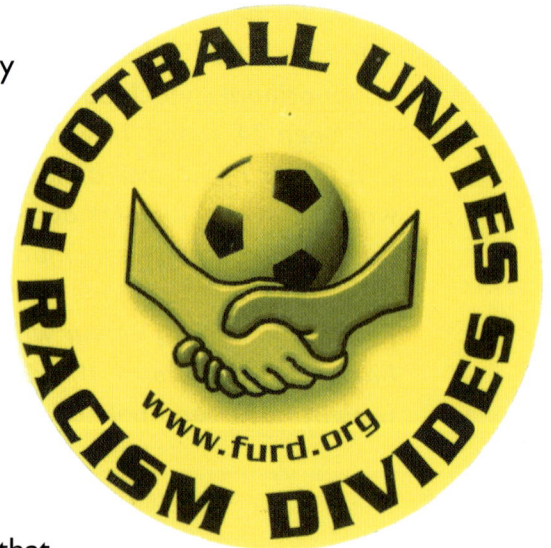

- Look at FURD's website. What are their aims?

- What practical things are they doing to combat racism?

- Divide into groups to look at the work of FARE – Football Against Racism in Europe; 'Show Racism the Red Card'; FURD; and 'Kick it Out'. All have web-sites you can consult. Report back to the class on what has been achieved.

Unit 8   *feedback*

UNITED COLORS OF BENETTON.

1   This advert caused offence. What is the hidden message in the picture? Do you think anyone would have objected if the roles had been reversed? Why?
With a partner, study the adverts in three different magazines, or in an evening's television. Are there any you think could cause offence to groups of people (women, men, ethnic minorities, old people, gay people, children)? Why?

2   Choose an image from a magazine to be central to an anti-racism poster for a pub or sports club. Design a poster that will make people stop and think about racism. You will need a snappy slogan and a logo.

3   Stephen Lawrence's mother said:

> If those who had murdered my son had been better educated in knowing who had helped to build this society in which we live they would have realised that everything in this country has black people who have played a part in it. We have helped to make the National Health Service what it is today, we have good transport, you name it and we have been a part of it. We have more than earned our place to live and not to have our children killed in the way that Stephen was.

Give three practical recommendations you could make to the headteacher in your school that would improve the teaching and learning about racism.

4   What text message about racism would you send to football supporters, and why?

5   Find out more about the work of the Catholic Association for Racial Justice. Why might a Christian believe this is the sort of work they should get involved in?

I've got my rights

With a partner, discuss what rights you think you have:

- to decent housing – what if you don't pay the rent?

- if you are arrested by the police

- to receive an education – up to what age? for free?

- to a job – for life? one you like?

- to be safe – where? when?

- In the 21st century, two-thirds of the world's governments use torture – not to gain information but either because of a person's beliefs, or because of who they are.

- 'Washing one's hands of the conflict between the powerful and the powerless means to side with the powerful, not to be neutral.' (*Paulo Friere, Brazil*)

- 'If you do not care for the afflictions of others, you do not deserve to be called a human being.' (*Sadi, a Persian Sufi poet*)

9.1 Who says?

Human beings are born free, equal and have rights.

- When do you think this was written? In which country? (See page 84 for the answer.)

In 1948, following human rights abuses in the Second World War, the United Nations drew up this declaration. The full text of it can be read on the United Nations website, but here are the main points.

The Universal Declaration of Human Rights

1 Right to equality
2 Freedom from discrimination
3 Right to life, liberty and personal security
4 Freedom from slavery
5 Freedom from torture or degrading treatment
6 Right to be recognised as a person by the law
7 Right to equality before the law
8 Right to a fair hearing if your rights are broken
9 Freedom from arrest with no reason, and exile
10 Right to a fair public hearing if accused of something illegal
11 Right to be considered innocent until proven guilty
12 Freedom from interference with privacy, family, home and correspondence
13 Right to free movement in and out of the country
14 Right to asylum in other countries if being persecuted at home
15 Right to a nationality and the freedom to change it
16 Right to marriage and family
17 Right to own property
18 Freedom of belief and religion
19 Freedom of opinion and information
20 Right to meet peacefully with others and join groups
21 Right to participate in government by voting and standing for election
22 Right to social security
23 Right to work safely for equal pay and to join a trade union
24 Right to rest and leisure
25 Right to an adequate living standard
26 Right to an education
27 Right to participate in cultural activities, e.g. the arts
28 Right to have society run in a way that protects your rights
29 Everyone has duties but these should only help achieve everyone's rights in society; they cannot harm rights
30 Everyone should be free from interference in their rights

OUTRAGE AS MOTHER'S BANNED FROM HITTING DAUGHTER

Are any human rights involved in this story? Do you think this sort of thing should be covered by law? What sort of punishment, if any, is acceptable for a parent to use on their child? Should anyone else be allowed to punish a child? Do you think it's okay for someone to slap their partner if they are provoked? Why?

PRISONER HANDCUFFED TO HOSPITAL BED AS SHE GIVES BIRTH

Why do you think this happened? What might the woman have done if she had not been handcuffed? Is this is a breach of human rights? Why?

Religious dad in court to stop hospital giving son blood transfusion

Should you be free to belong to any religion you like? Are you free to decide what is right for your child? What reasons might the father give for refusing his child a blood transfusion? How much notice should you take of the child's views on this? Who do you think should have the final say in this case – father, son, hospital or court? Why?

- Look back at the terms of the UN Declaration of the Rights of the Child on page 20. What differences can you see between this and the Declaration of Human Rights?

- Why do you think it was necessary to have them both?

Religious responses to human rights abuse

One very influential religious campaigner for human rights was the English priest Archbishop Trevor Huddleston. He fought for blacks to be given equal rights to whites in South Africa because, he said, 'I believed most strongly that fighting apartheid was a moral battle against something profoundly evil. It didn't come to me through academic reading or study. It came to me through seeing apartheid and its impact on the people whom I had responsibility for as a priest.'

Gandhi, an Indian, first began campaigning for equal rights for black people in South Africa. On his return to India he worked to end British control of the country and to return rights to the Indians. Although he was a Hindu, Gandhi had enormous respect for all religions and understood that all championed human rights. He is one of the greatest human rights leaders to promote non-violent protest.

- Malcolm X was a Muslim campaigner for equal rights in America. Find out about his activities and make a poster comparing his work with that of Martin Luther King.

> Open your newspaper – any day of the week – and you will find a report from somewhere in the world of someone being imprisoned, tortured or executed because his opinions or religion are unacceptable to his government. The newspaper reader feels a sickening sense of impotence. Yet if these feelings of disgust all over the world could be united into common action, something effective could be done. I was spurred into that by reading an article about how two Portuguese students had been arrested and sentenced to imprisonment for drinking a toast to liberty in a Lisbon restaurant. That so enraged me at the time that I walked up the steps of St Martin's-in-the-Fields church out of the Underground, and went in to see what could really be done effectively to mobilise world opinion.
> (Peter Benenson)

- Look on Amnesty's website and list five areas they are currently concerned about. These could be places or issues.

In 1961, a Christian called Peter Benenson was so disgusted by the abuse of human rights that he did something. He founded Amnesty International. It is not specifically a Christian charity – Amnesty International helps people of any religion, colour or race who are imprisoned or tortured because of their beliefs. The candle in Amnesty's logo is surrounded by barbed wire. Benenson said, 'The candle burns not for us, but for all those whom we failed to rescue from prison, who were shot on the way to prison, who were tortured, who were kidnapped, who "disappeared".'

What connection do these people have with the Universal Declaration of Human Rights? What does the term 'asylum-seeker' mean? What does an asylum-seeker have to prove to the Home Office officials before they can be allowed to stay?

In Britain today we like to think we have a tolerant attitude and that human rights abuses are something which happen in far-off places.

Work in groups of three or four

1   Name two or three minority groups in this country that are discriminated against.

2   Why? How do people regard them?

3   List four institutions, or types of people, who might treat them as inferior.

4   Look back to page 78 and list all the rights defined in the UN Declaration of Human Rights that are being violated.

Imagine that your publicity company has been asked to work on an advertising campaign on behalf of one of these minority groups: The money has been put up by a charity that is concerned about human rights abuse. Expensive though it will be, the charity thinks that this is the most effective way of helping the group. How do you feel about that?

The brief

- Plan a 3-minute TV advert, or a set of four different posters to be displayed in big cities.

- You need to show that there is good in these people.

- You have to explain why they deserve to be given equal rights.

Asylum applications
Number of applications (including dependants), 2001

Country	Applications	Per 1,000
Germany	88,365	1.1
UK	88,300	1.5
France	53,875	0.9
Netherlands	32,580	2.0
Austria	30,135	3.7
Belgium	27,960	2.7
Sweden	23,500	2.7
Switzerland	20,770	2.9
Norway	14,780	3.3
Denmark	12,405	2.3
Ireland	10,325	2.7
European Union	388,770	1.1

1.5 Applications per 1,000 population

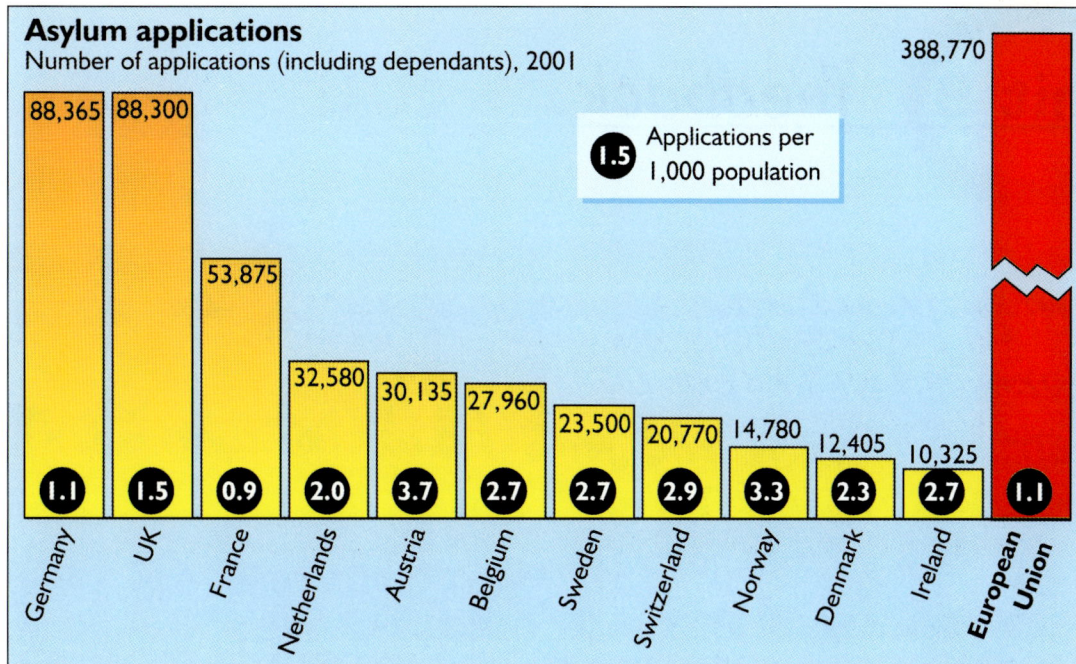

What does the graph above show about the popularity of Britain as a destination? Research the total population of each country listed here. Which is receiving the largest number of asylum-seekers in relation to its total population?

In 2001, asylum-seekers to Britain were made up of:

9,190 from Afghanistan

6,805 from Iraq

6,500 from Somalia

5,545 from Sri Lanka

3,740 from Turkey

- Cross-check with Amnesty's website to see if any human rights abuses have been recorded in these countries, and report back.

- Can you discover any political reasons for people wanting to leave these countries?

First they came for the communists and I did not speak out - because I was not a communist
Then they came for the Jews I did not speak out because I was not a Jew
Then they came for the trade unionionists and I did not speak out
because I was not a trade unionist
Next they came for the Catholics and I did not speak out because I was not a Catholic
Then they came for me and there was no one left to speak out for me

This was written by Martin Niemöller, a Protestant minister who campaigned against Hitler's human rights abuse during the Second World War. Niemöller was captured by the Nazis and put in a concentration camp, but he survived.

1   After reading Niemöller's words, discuss as a class whether it does make a difference if people speak out. Can you think of any modern-day parallels anywhere in the world? Is bullying linked with this?

2   Write a 21st-century version of Niemöller's words. It can relate to anywhere in the world.

3   Go through a daily newspaper and cut out all the stories relating to some form of human rights abuse. In your exercise book make a brief note of the case and against each write which particular point or points of the Universal Declaration of Human Rights was being infringed.

> The answer to the quotation on page 78, 'Human beings are born free, equal and have rights', is that it was part of the French constitution established in 1789 after the French Revolution.

Spend, spend, spend! Unit 10

- 'IF YOU'VE GOT IT, SPLASH IT AROUND!' (*Lottery winner*)
- 'You can't serve both God and money.' (*Matthew 6:24*)
- Jesus said: 'If you want to be perfect, go and sell all you have and give the money to the poor, and you will have riches in heaven; then come and follow me.' (*Matthew 19:21*)
- Who wants to be a millionaire?

- Tourism is set to become the world's largest industry.
- By 2015 it is thought there will be 1.3 billion tourists travelling every year.
- One long-haul flight uses as much fuel as a small car does in a year.
- The three richest people on the planet have more wealth than its 600 million poorest inhabitants.

10.1 What's wrong with money?

There is nothing wrong with money. In fact we wouldn't get far if we didn't have any.

Look at the following quotations from Christian scriptures and work out what Jesus said about money and its use. How realistic do you think his teachings are in the 21st century? Why?

Jesus said:

> Your heart will always be where your riches are. (*Matthew 6:21*)

- What implication would this have for Christians putting their money in a bank that makes loans to a country known for its human rights abuse? What else could the quotation mean?

> Watch out and guard yourselves from every kind of greed; because a person's true life is not made up of the things he owns, no matter how rich he may be. (*Luke 12:15*)

- What is meant by this? If it is not what you own that matters – then what is it?

> Much is required from the person to whom much is given; much more is required from the person to whom much more is given. (*Luke 12:48*)

- What are the implications of this statement for someone like Brooklyn Beckham?

Does money cause problems?

Do you think there are any dangers in spending money this way? Or is it just a harmless piece of fun? What do you think will happen to the player's winnings? As a class, discuss whether you agree with the saying 'Money is the root of all evil'.

Stacey

The church choir went carol-singing last Christmas to collect for the children's hospice. We went round loads of pubs and restaurants and it was really interesting to watch people's reactions. There was one bloke. He was smartly dressed, all expensive designer stuff. His plate was piled high with food. It was quite obvious he wasn't pushed for a penny. Do you know, he put his hand in his pocket and drew out a load of pound and two-pound coins, then he sifted through and took a couple of two pence pieces to chuck in our collecting bucket. I was disgusted. On the Thursday we sang at a few old people's homes to cheer them up and give them a bit of Christmas spirit. The old dears there were the opposite. They insisted on giving us £5, that sort of thing. It was really weird. I didn't want to take it but they insisted, saying it was for a good cause.

- Read the story of the poor widow in Luke 21:1–4. Do you think there is any similarity with the story above? Or would you say it is totally different? Why?

- Find out about CAF from their website. What does CAF stand for? How is it that the organisation receives more money than the person actually donates?

With a partner

1 Role-play the scene in the restaurant between Stacey and the rich diner. What reasons does he give for his donation?

2 Create four designs for beer mats that could be put in pubs and restaurants by the children's hospice to encourage giving.

3 What do you think is the best way for the charity to collect those donations? Are you happy about people collecting for charity in the street or in restaurants? Why?

10.2 The holiday of a lifetime? Or food for thought?

The chances are that if you won a large amount of money, you would take the holiday of a lifetime. Who wouldn't? Where would you go? Choosing might not be quite as easy as it sounds if you were to consider the impact of the holiday on the environment or on the local people.

With a partner

Decide on your dream holiday, where money is no object. Where would you go? How would you get there? What would you do?

Now think about these points:

- Who owns the airplane you will be travelling on?

- Where will you be staying? If it is a hotel, is it part of a chain that is owned by a foreign company?

- When you are away, will you eat local food or luxury foods that have to be imported?

- Would you be tempted by an 'all-inclusive deal' where everything is paid for before you leave home, and no food, drink, tours or entertainment needs paying for locally?

- Would you feel comfortable staying in an expensive hotel where the amount you spent in the bar during an evening could feed a local family for a week? Why?

We are committed to giving our customers the lowest possible prices!

We've worked hard all year so we deserve this break.

I've always wanted to travel and see how the rest of the world lives. We've booked a trip on an elephant to see a native village. And we're going to stay the night in one of their huts. We'll have a good time and they get the money.

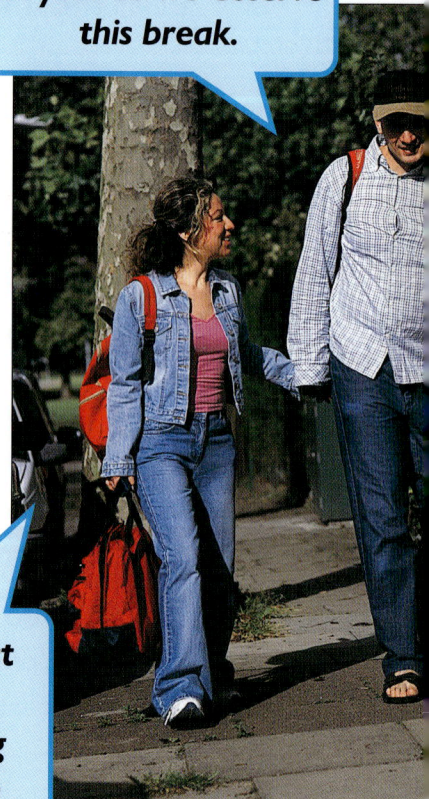

88

> *We feel invaded when they come. They don't understand our ways. They touch sacred objects they shouldn't and they walk around our streets in bikinis and shorts, which is a bad influence on my children.*

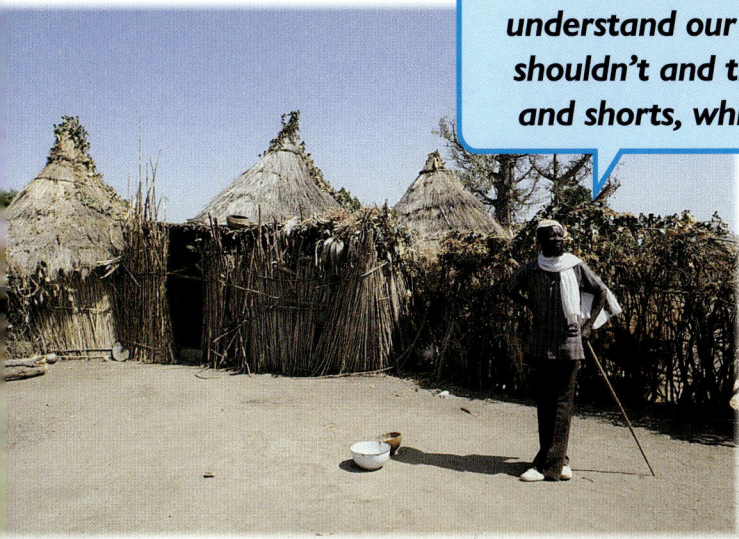

Do you think he has got a point or should he be grateful for the business? What would you say in reply to him?

A big hotel built in a protected forest in Kenya diverted the area's small river to provide water. This caused the water, which normally ran down into the local village most of the year, to dry up almost completely. This resulted in a lack of vegetation downstream as well as a lack of water for people and animals. The community was very upset with the owners of the hotel and also couldn't understand how they got a permit to build on their land without their involvement. The hotel owners have started providing a bit of development help, such as a school and road repairs, in order to appease them and defuse their anger, but it doesn't solve the water problems.

Mama Ceesay sold eggs under the hot sun in Serekunda market near the main tourist area in The Gambia. She had done it for years and never made much money until she was helped by a Voluntary Services Overseas small business adviser to get involved in local tourism. As a result a neighbouring hotel began buying her eggs and she doubled her earnings overnight. Today Mama owns 5,000 hens and a new home, and pays for the education of her three children. (*Voluntary Services Overseas – VSO*)

- Look on the VSO website to see what problems and what advantages tourism can bring.

- Design a double-sided A5 leaflet that could be put inside a travel brochure asking tourists to consider these issues when booking their holiday.

The Trade Justice Movement

This is a scene from the Trade Justice Parade in London in 2001. Over 8,000 people marched from Lambeth to Trafalgar Square calling for fairer rules for the way that international trade is carried out. There were giant puppets, floats and bands to get the message across. Fat Cats in bloated business suits proved the most popular fancy dress! There was also an army of white-coated doctors who carried mock packets of pills labelled 'to be kept out of the reach of poor people'.

What is the problem?

Many Christians, along with people of other faiths, are concerned that the rich nations of the world are exploiting the poorer nations. (If you look back to page 38 you can see the effect the rich nations can have on working conditions in the clothing industry.) The United Nations estimate that the developing countries lose 700 billion dollars every year because of unfair trade rules. That is seven times as much money as they are given in aid. The result is that the poor are getting poorer and the rich, richer.

- Investigate the progress of this campaign on the website of the Trade Justice Movement. Or look at the work of specific charities in this area like Christian Aid, CAFOD, Oxfam and Friends of the Earth.

- Is this campaign restricted to the UK? Are members of other religions taking part? Friends of the Earth are not a religious group, so why do you think they are concerned about this problem?

International trade is governed by a set of rules

But the rules are designed to protect the wealthy – and it's poor people who are paying the price

This prayer was written for use during a campaign for fair trade.

Tilt the scales

O God of the mustard seed:

That the poor shall see justice.

Share the feast,

O God of Eden's abundant garden:

That each crop may fetch a fair price.

Upset the tables,

O God of the upside-down Kingdom:

That the least can benefit from their trade.

Open our eyes,

O God of life in all its fullness:

That we may learn to walk the way of your son

Tilting, sharing, upsetting this world

Not satisfied until the products we bring to our table

Give a better deal, to all who hunger for one.

In His name, Amen. (*CAFOD*)

● Look at Mary's words before the birth of Jesus in Luke 1:51–53. How does that match the ideas in this prayer?

Unit 10 *feedback*

What on earth are you going to do?

1   Design a postcard that the Trade Justice Movement could use to send to politicians and officials connected with world trade, urging them to deal fairly with the developing world. What image and snappy message would it carry on the front? One idea used in the past, when 35,000 postcards cards were sent, showed a pair of dice, one of which was loaded – you can guess who the big heavy dice represented! The picture above shows another card design used recently.

With a partner

2   Try to work out what was meant by these words spoken by Sir Walter Raleigh: 'Whoever commands the trade of the world commands the riches of the world and hence the world itself.' Share your ideas as a class.

3   Read the famous teachings of Jesus on the Sermon on the Mount in Matthew 5:3–12 Write a modern version that might apply to those living in the developing countries.

4   Using publicity material collected from one or more of the charities concerned in the Trade Justice Movement, arrange a display to inform pupils of the campaign.

5   Investigate what 'ethical banking' means. Triodos Bank, established in 1980 in the Netherlands, says: 'We only lend money to businesses, projects and charitable initiatives delivering real social, environmental and cultural benefits. We don't just avoid enterprises that do harm. We positively choose to finance only those which actively do good.'

Give three examples of projects you think they might support, and three they would not agree with. Look on their website to see what they are currently supporting. Why might Christians or Buddhists choose this sort of bank? Find out the views of a leading high street bank on ethical banking.

Top 10 Tips for Citizenship projects

Tip 1 Do something you are interested in

Try to find a topic that interests you, that you feel you can widen or narrow down, concerned with something you have a keen interest in. You don't want to be bored. It would be great if what you did proved useful to you outside school or in the future.

Tip 2 Get involved

- You could organise a class debate around some issues. This needs setting up properly with a chairperson who is fair and can keep everyone in order. You will need two speakers *for*, and two *against*, the motion. It is the chairperson's job to make sure everyone gets time to speak and that the audience get a chance to question or comment on the motion before voting.

- If your project involves something you care about greatly, then you want people to know. You will need to raise awareness by publicising information. Investigate the use of noticeboards. Think about holding a school assembly or publishing a newsletter. Consider taking your project out into the community – think big!

Tip 3 Co-ordinate what you're doing with your school

You should keep your teacher informed about what you are doing, even if some of your activities take place in your own time. Your teacher can help you plan the next stage of your work, and can also smooth your way by allowing you to keep appointments during school time, or suggesting contacts for you.

Tip 4 Plan your project

The chances are that you are not working on your own. Bouncing ideas off others in the group is useful and fun. Everyone has different skills, so use them to everyone's advantage. Once the topic is settled, get the group sorted. Plan the order in which you intend to do the work, and define exactly what everyone is going to do to ensure the best use of time and people.

Tip 5 Get your facts right

Don't rely totally on one source of information. An important skill to develop as you work through your Citizenship project is that of sifting information. An incident can be reported in newspapers or magazines in quite different ways. The reporters may not actually be telling lies but they might have put a different 'slant' or 'spin' on the facts. Parts of the story might be left out or deliberately exaggerated to influence your opinion. When you are using reports or statistics, if possible check another account to see if anyone is trying to bias your thinking. Copy down facts and figures carefully. With any facts and figures you should include the source, written below. No one takes things seriously unless they know how reliable the information is. 'Prove it!' – that's what you are likely to hear. So make sure you can!

Tip 6 Getting skilled

The work you do will challenge you. Along the way you will learn a lot of new facts but perhaps more importantly you will learn how to do things. Keep a note of the new skills you learn. A future employer will be interested to know.

If your work is worthwhile you need to keep a record of everything you did. Notes in a folder are a help but it is useful to fill in a spreadsheet or table regularly to keep track of where and when you did your research and, briefly, what you found out. This can be kept on computer or on paper.

Tip 7 *Make it worthwhile*

It is so much more satisfying to know that what you are doing is worthwhile for both you and others in the community. Citizenship is about more than working through exercises in a book. The idea is that when you have finished, you will have gained something yourself and hopefully made your mark – in the nicest way! – on society. It might be that you got involved in a project to improve conditions for children at a local playgroup; persuaded the local council to start a doorstep recycling scheme; started a counselling service in the upper school; raised money to begin … the ideas are endless.

Tip 8 *The good questionnaire*

Often it is useful to discover the views of a group of people on an issue. A survey or questionnaire is ideal.

- Before you start, define in one sentence basically what it is you want to know.

- What sort of sample will you need for the survey to be representative? Gender/age/number asked?

- Keep the questions simple and unambiguous. Don't 'lead' with questions like 'Just how great do you think X is?'

- For ease of working, design 'closed' questions that can be answered by *Yes*, *No* or *Don't know*. Another useful method is to ask people to rate their response to your questions on a scale of 1 to 5. Don't forget to tell them about the scale, e.g.

'On a scale of 1 to 5, where 1 is *Very good* and 5 is *Very bad* …'.

- Be careful not to ask anything offensive, intrusive or personal.

- You need to be able to display the results as a graph or diagram. Decide how you will analyse them.

- How are you going to make your questionnaire/survey look professional?

Tip 9 *Press release*

- Keep it brief and to the point!

- Make sure that you get your main point over in the first sentence, because if you don't grab people's attention immediately nobody will read any further.

- Use four points to back up your main point.

- Include some proof/clear evidence/facts that are true and interesting and could interest a reporter.

Tip 10 *Interviewing*

- Remember: people are doing you a favour. They probably don't have to talk to you, so be polite and don't waste their time.

- Work out a whole series of questions (20 perhaps), or headings of topics, so that you know what you are trying to find out.

- Be flexible. If an interesting point arises don't be afraid to follow it up even if it wasn't on your list. Don't stick to the list rigidly. If the person has answered that point already, don't ask it again.

- Tape-record or make notes of what was said. If you work in pairs, one can interview and one record the information.

- Decide before you begin how you will later use, or evaluate, the content of the interview.

Index